Courageous Learners: Unleashing the Brain Power of Students from At-Risk Situations

Donna Wilson, Ph.D.

&

Marcus Conyers

Layout design: Lorraine Holden
Cover design: Erika Amlund
Interior graphics: Rob Van Tol
Editing: Jeanne Zehr
Word processing: Leslie Wilson

www.brainsmart.com

Contents

Donna Wilson, Ph.D.

Donna Wilson, former university faculty and chair, is a leader in the development of brain friendly learning systems grounded in cognitive education. Donna is a school psychologist, consultant, and author specializing in the creation of learning and thinking schools. She has presented to thousands of educators throughout the U.S. and Canada, including many of the largest districts in the U.S. such as St. Louis, New York City, Chicago, Los Angeles, Dallas, Orlando, and many more.

Donna has conducted research in applied cognitive education, health care, and reading with children and while working as a professor received a major grant from BellSouth for a model teacher induction program. Donna has produced video and audio tapes and other books including *BrainSMART Strategies for Boosting Test Scores* (2000) and *BrainSMART In the House: Learning for School Learning for Life* (in press, a) with Marcus Conyers. Soon to be released is their BrainSMART video series, tapes for teachers and tapes for parents.

Marcus Conyers "The Brain Guy"

Marcus Conyers, international author and researcher, is a leading pioneer in translating implications of brain research into tools for boosting learning and teaching. He spent over 25 years in 35 countries developing BrainSMART, a research based system for boosting student achievement grounded in how neuroscience suggests the human brain naturally learns best. Marcus has also inspired millions by his appearances on more than 600 TV and radio shows around the world.

Marcus has taught BrainSMART to 30,000 teachers, students, corporate trainers, and university faculty around the world. The system has been chosen by the Florida Department of Education for a three year state wide "train the trainer" initiative for promoting dropout prevention. He is one of the most dynamic keynoters in education today. Other books by Marcus include *BrainSMART Strategies* (2000), *BrainSMART Early Start* (1999), *Peak Performance Radiant Health* (2000), and *Speed Reading the Easy Way* (1997).

Special Thank You to the National Staff Development Council

The trigger for the writing of this book was the National Staff Development Council annual conference in Dallas, Texas in 1999. We appreciated the positive comments that we received about our workshops. We were uncomfortable, however, about the fact that we had not done enough to bring home a crucial point. The fact is that there is an urgent need to plan professional development differently to reach the exploding number of students in our schools who do not benefit as well from standard teaching practice.

In particular the at-risk label concerned us at it often precipitated four deadly approaches to teaching such students that research suggests will put students at great risk of academic failure.

- Retaining students a grade and repeating the same instruction
- Putting students into ability groups
- Increased use of ditto sheets and test prep teaching approaches rather than methods using higher order thinking and hands-on teaching
- Avoiding sustained collaboration with parents and guardians who are responsible for 87% of student waking hours

Donna heard NSDC Executive Director Dennis Sparks (NSDC Donference 1999) speak of the priority the NSDC is placing on reaching students from at-risk situations. We were inspired to get to work and complete this **pilot** edition of *Courageous Learners* for the 2000 conference. We were delighted when our application to present *Courageous Learners* at NSDC in 2000 Atlanta was approved and thrilled that people from 30 states booked in advance, selling out the workshop six weeks before the conference.

We agree fully with the NSDC that teachers must have significant amounts of time to develop their teaching practice within their own learning communities. When working in Japan, Marcus was struck by the high level of education demonstrated by Japanese citizens. It was interesting to read in *The Learning Gap* that elementary teachers in Japan have up to 40% of their time each day available to meet with colleagues, plan lessons and increase their capacity to teach effectively. We believe that teaching is applied cognitive neuroscience, and that teachers in all countries deserve the training, time, and support they need to be successful in such an important profession.

This book is designed to support professional developers and learning communities with research and ideas that will enhance the professional development of teachers of courageous learners. We do not suggest that the NSDC shares the views expressed in this book. We do, however, thank the NSDC and the membership for all you are doing to enhance the lives of children by ensuring that they are taught the thinking and learning tools they need to be successful in school and in life. Most importantly, we thank you, the reader, for being a courageous learner, willing to risk leaving the safety of rhetoric for the journey of modeling in your every day actions the ways of teaching effectively in the 21st century. You are truly a gift.

Donna Wilson and Marcus Conyers

Courageous Introduction

TEACHING IS A PROFESSION. TEACHING IS APPLIED COGNITIVE NEUROSCIENCE. THEREFORE, TEACHERS NEED THE TRAINING, TIME, AND COMPENSATION THAT SUCH A NOBLE AND IMPORTANT PROFESSION REQUIRES.

Overview

One of the most exhilarating experiences in life is to see courageous learners feel the full power and joy of achieving academic success. In classrooms across North America and around the world we have been humbled and inspired at what great teachers do to change their teaching practice in ways that dramatically increase student learning. At the same time we have witnessed the impact of courageous leadership in creating the opportunities for teachers to learn the best practices that work for students from adverse situations. For example, in Florida, Mary Jo Butler and Nancy Romain supported our three year project in training a cadre of teachers in the BrainSMART Model for translating brain and cognitive research into tools for effective teaching.

The explosion in brain research has resulted in a situation where 90% of what we know about the brain has been learned in the last ten years. For example, the Society of Neuroscience has blossomed from around 500 members in the seventies to more than 30,000 members today with an average age of thirty-two. Perhaps the most exciting aspect of this explosion in research is that it supports fifty years of research in the cognitive sciences concerning what it takes to teach students to think, learn, communicate, and achieve success in school and in life. Author Donna has had the privilege of working with Dr. Reuven Feuerstein in Israel. Feuerstein (1980) pioneered work with children who were survivors of the Holocaust after the Second World War. He found that by teaching a specific system of thinking and learning, a student's capacity to think, learn, and grow could be dramatically improved. Donna, a former teacher, school psychologist, and university faculty member, has now developed a powerful next phase in this work that is particularly appropriate for students in North American Schools. So it is with great excitement that we share with you our lives' work to-date in this book *Courageous Learners*. We hope that you will join us as part of the growing network of individuals committed to truly encouraging the academic and life long success of all students. If our last fifty years of research indicate one thing, it is that it is possible for most all students to learn if two basic conditions are met:

1) Students must be taught the specific thinking, learning, and communication skills that they need to be successful in school. If students arrive in the classroom without these skills, we must make sure that they get the necessary help to acquire them if we are serious about all students becoming successful, and

2) Teachers must be given the training, tools, and time to learn how to teach in ways in which all students can be successful.

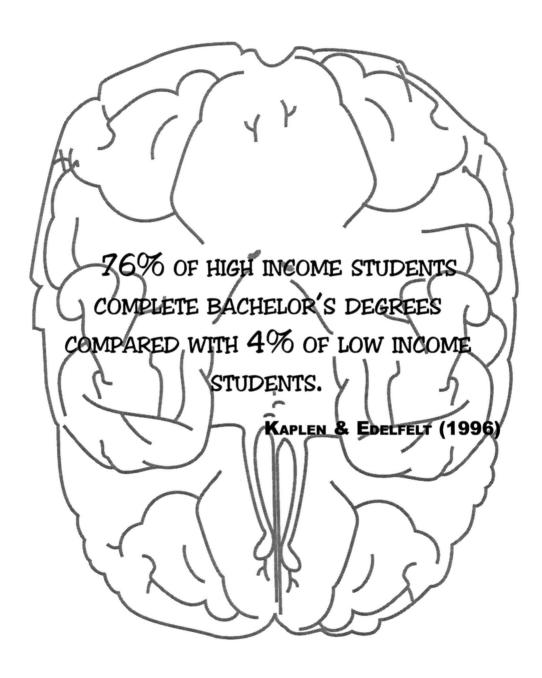

76% OF HIGH INCOME STUDENTS COMPLETE BACHELOR'S DEGREES COMPARED WITH 4% OF LOW INCOME STUDENTS.

KAPLEN & EDELFELT (1996)

At the dawn of the twenty first century we must realize a powerful truth about teaching and learning. **Teaching is applied cognitive neuroscience.** Teachers need and deserve the training and compensation appropriate for such a critically important profession. It is only when we fundamentally change the system of teaching that we can truly give courageous learners the education they deserve to unleash their limitless potential. As you journey with us through this book, our hope is that you will be equipped with the latest information on how we can help our courageous learners become more successful. May you be encouraged by our many stories of how courageous learners and teachers have made it work in the real world, and inspired to take action within your own school or school system.

Outline of Chapters

"Courageous Learners - Individuals who courageously work at overcoming the situations that put them at-risk of academic failure"

The authors, Donna Wilson and Marcus Conyers, have worked with over 30,000 teachers and thousands of children and youth throughout the U.S. and Canada, many of whom are courageous learners. Bringing an international perspective and a broad range of experience, authors Donna and Marcus highlight the fact that there is an emergency in U.S. education today. Seventy-five percent of students do not learn well by frequently used methods of instruction. The academic failure of many students is likely to worsen despite the best efforts of teachers and students.

In his book, *The New Economics,* Deming (1994) states that 94% of problems are produced by the system and 6% by special causes. Despite the efforts by many caring teachers, the existing system is putting millions of students at-risk of academic failure. At the same time, exciting breakthroughs in brain and cognitive research, when translated into tools for effective teaching, are showing great promise. The purpose of this book is to provide a road map and tools to help educators and administrators transform the system so that all students can learn.

Chapter 1:   Ten Key Facts About C.O.U.R.A.G.E.O.U.S. Learners

In Chapters 1 - 3 we give an overview of research, facts, and issues that impact courageous learners. In Chapter 1, you may equip yourself with a powerful framework for understanding the potential for unleashing the brainpower of courageous learners. Learn the top ten insights about the ways that courageous learners learn and the barriers that may be putting them at-risk of academic failure.

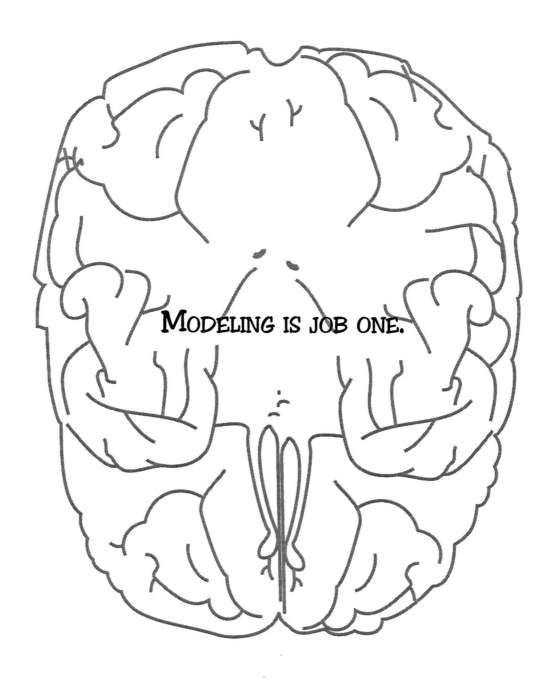

MODELING IS JOB ONE.

Since this is a BrainSMART™ book designed with learning in mind, the acronym C.O.U.R.A.G.E.O.U.S is used to help you retain, recall, and apply the insights you will learn. By the end of this chapter you may be able to discover opportunities for increasing the academic success of the students in your classroom, school or district. This chapter is also designed to be useful for professional developers or university faculty who wish to give an overview of some key issues that impact the academic and lifelong success of courageous learners.

Chapter 2: Translating Research to Results

Deepen your understanding of the major research findings about the situation facing students at-risk of academic failure. Develop a useful schema about the factors that have the most impact on academic success.

Learn answers to some critical questions. What is the impact of standard education practice on student achievement? Has standard teaching practice changed in recent years? Are the brains of students different today? What is the impact of the home environment on student achievement? What percentage of the content of a lecture will students remember after 24 hours? What is the impact of family income on SAT scores? Do college graduates really earn nearly 2 million dollars more than a high school dropout? What is the impact of stress on right hemispheric dominant students?

Chapter 3: Four Fundamental Forces of Learning

With clarity of mission that all students deserve to succeed, a system for meeting teacher and student needs is necessary. First, in order to prevent placing students in difficulty, we must ensure that all children acquire the thinking, learning, and communication tools to "innoculate" them against at-risk situations. Second, we must ensure that those students already identified as needing interventions are adequately served.

So then, what is it that all students do need to succeed? The BrainSMART Learning Forces Model for creating greater student learning and achievement is introduced, and courageous learners is positioned within the Learning Forces Model. The four necessary forces in this model are: Prenatal and pre-k, parental support, physical/psychological health and safety, and preparation and professional development of educators and mentors. Throughout the book authors Donna and Marcus note a broad research base, articulate principles, and suggest actions about the professional development of educators in schools where all students have an opportunity to learn and achieve.

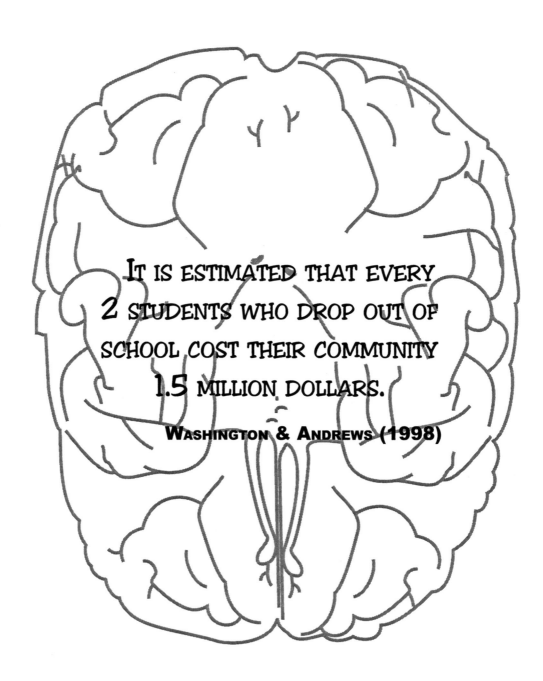

IT IS ESTIMATED THAT EVERY 2 STUDENTS WHO DROP OUT OF SCHOOL COST THEIR COMMUNITY 1.5 MILLION DOLLARS.

WASHINGTON & ANDREWS (1998)

BrainSMART Tools for Thinking and Learning

Research reported by the National Dropout Prevention Network indicates that four of five teachers do not think they are prepared to teach students today. Many of these teachers do not feel equipped to teach are those considered at-risk. These at-risk students comprise a growing number that have predictable characteristics. These students who have difficulty are usually right hemispheric dominant, making them learners who need to have overviews, summaries, and many real life examples, rather than fragmentation of learning. Second, they are visual and kinesthetic and tend to do very poorly with direct auditory instruction and worksheets. Third, many of these students have not had preparatory experiences in preschool that set them in motion for school success. Therefore, they must catch up on how to learn with a teacher as guide. Fourth, many at-risk students do not have the cognitive prerequisites for learning and need to learn them.

Chapters 4 - 6 are full of practical strategies that can be used by teachers of courageous learners immediately. Chapter 4 explains the coaching model as a framework for teaching thinking and gives 7 important tools for immediate use. In chapter 5 you will find an overview of the BrainSMART learning model and 19 practical strategies for increasing memory. In chapter 6 you will learn the Barcode for the Brain as a system for enhancing classroom communication.

Chapter 4:   BrainSMART Tools for Thinking

After practicing as a teacher, school psychologist, and professor for many years, Donna and others in the field have become convinced that at-risk learners need what she considers the prerequisites of good thinking. It is exciting to know that these can be developed in students after they enter school, as well as before.

In this chapter the authors consider the importance of relationships, guidance or coaching, and certain cognitive prerequisites that are necessary for school success. Students in at-risk situations often "fail school" due to a lack of self control, short attention span, lack of regard for others' space, poor planning ability, inability to organize their work, and poor communication skills. They are sometimes in difficulty because of pessimism, tardiness, poor anger control, and an inability to relate. What we have found most interesting is that these prerequisites for thinking are not explicitly taught in traditional schools. Consider, with Donna and Marcus, the seven prerequisites for thinking and use the ideas that have worked to increase student learning and achievement!

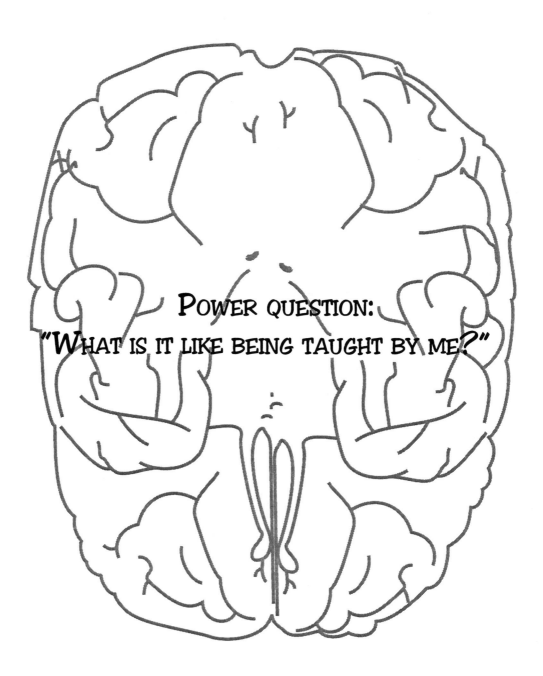

POWER QUESTION:
"WHAT IS IT LIKE BEING TAUGHT BY ME?"

Chapter 5:   BrainSMART Tools for Learning

In this chapter authors Marcus and Donna will introduce five fundamental principles for facilitating student learning (Conyers & Wilson, 2000). They are as follows: 1) *state*, how to trigger and sustain the neurophysiology of peak learning states; 2) *meaning*, how to make learning meaningful and relevant for all students; 3) *attention*, how to sustain laser sharp attention balanced with powerful reflection and feedback strategies; *4) retention*, how to ensure that important information is quickly stored into long-term memory; and *5) transfer*, how to ensure that what is learned in the classroom is recalled during tests and in life. After a brief introduction of the core BrainSMART principles, this chapter is devoted to equipping students with a toolbox of highly effective strategies for enhancing retention, recall, and results. In our work with students in at-risk situations we have found that concrete experiences of success in this area yield a profound and lasting shift in their feeling of competence about learning.

Courageous learners Donna and Marcus have enjoyed meeting in the classroom often have impressive strengths in the visual - kinesthetic modalities. The last 3,000 students we have worked with have consistently demonstrated 100% recall of material presented to them using BrainSMART strategies, appropriate for visual - kinesthetic modality strong learners. As we have marveled at the high levels of skill and commitment demonstrated by teachers, we have found agreement with the BrainSMART principle, "it's never lack of ability it's always lack of strategy." In this chapter Donna and Marcus share the exhilarating experience of the BrainSMART learning and teaching system that has helped many teachers reach students who are hard to reach.

Chapter 6:   BrainSMART Barcode for the Brain

Discover a powerful process for beginning to read your students like a book; building positive rapport; and influencing with integrity. The Barcode for the Brain process, first developed by the authors for use by counter intelligence officers, is consistently one of the most popular tools that participants learn in the 5 day institutes. This process is useful not only in the classroom, but also for understanding, predicting and motivating desired behaviors in others in all aspects of your personal and professional life.

Learn how to read the 7 S.T.R.I.P.E.S of the learning brain so that you can teach in ways that maximize the success of the courageous learners in your classroom. Uncover the hidden reasons for many of the personality conflicts that may disrupt positive relationships with your students. Develop your ability to use forms of communication that positively motivate productive learning in your classroom.

THE IMPACT OF HOUSEHOLD INCOME ON S.A.T. SCORES

Less than $10,000	873
$10,000 - $20,000	918
$20,000 - $30,000	972
$30,000 - $40,000	993
$40,000 - $50,000	1015
$50,000 - $60,000	1033
$60,000 - $70,000	1048
$70,000 - $80,000	1062
$80,000 - $100,000	1084
Above $100,000	1130

ADAPTED FROM
THE SCHOOLS OUR CHILDREN DESERVE
BY ALFIE KOHN (1999)

Chapter 7:   Inspiring Examples: Stories from District and State Initiatives

Authors Marcus and Donna share two powerful examples of schools and state departments working courageously to serve all students better. First, author Marcus shares the S.T.A.R. story and tells of this ongoing 3 year initiative by the State Department of Education in Florida. This project was put in place 3 years ago in order to decrease the number of students dropping out in the state of Florida.

Second, a model that author Donna has used is brought to life through the real world example of a project in Oklahoma (Wilson & Church, 1993). Designed by a suburban school district to better serve all students, this project further integrates special and regular education services. Students and teachers are provided powerful methods to ensure that all at-risk students have their learning needs met. Both of these stories are told to illustrate the courage in schools across the U.S. as they attempt to educate students whose needs are changing rapidly.

Chapter 8:   "True North" Principles for Teaching Courageous Learners

In this chapter authors Donna and Marcus outline the steps for continuing the professional developmentprocess for students in at-risk situations through an understanding of the reality of the change process. First, remember the Pareto Principle discussed in Koch's (1998) book *The 20/80 Principle*. This powerful principal is that 20% of action produces 80% of results. Second, keep in mind that school change takes three years for elementary, six years for high school, and eight years for the district. Third, remember that every successful school reform has focused on student learning and achievement as the primary goal. Lastly, give teachers professional development, time, and support to transform instruction to meet the needs of today's students.

Chapter 1
Ten Key Facts About C.O.U.R.A.G.E.O.U.S. Learners

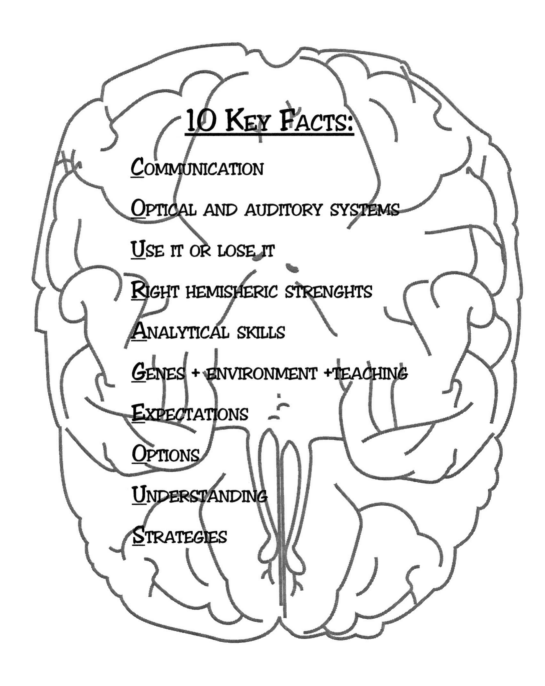

10 KEY FACTS:

COMMUNICATION

OPTICAL AND AUDITORY SYSTEMS

USE IT OR LOSE IT

RIGHT HEMISHERIC STRENGHTS

ANALYTICAL SKILLS

GENES + ENVIRONMENT + TEACHING

EXPECTATIONS

OPTIONS

UNDERSTANDING

STRATEGIES

Brain and cognitive research suggest the following 10 key facts for improving the success of courageous learners.

We will use the acronym C.O.U.R.A.G.E.O.U.S to help you retain, recall and apply this information. The Courageous frame of thinking will help you get the most out of this book!

<u>C</u> ommunication Constructs the Brain

The human brain craves communication. Research cited in *BrainSMART Early Start* (Conyers & Heverly, 1999) indicates that the more language experience students have at home, the better they are likely to do at school. Language may boost the left hemispheric regions including the Broca and Wernicke areas. The orbitofrontal area which is involved in the integration of language, and the basal ganglia area which is associated with bonding are central to the process of communication..

Facts

- Children of welfare families have 13 million words less language experience by age 4 than contemporaries from middle class families.

- Such children start school with 50% less vocabulary

- Children who read well have had 1,000 hours of cumulative language experience before they start school.

- Time spent positively communicating with parents is the best way to reduce the risk of suicide, aggression and drug abuse.

- Parents today are spending 30% less time with their children than a decade ago.

Action

Ensure that children have intensive language remediation to offset any shortfall in preschool language experience. Ensure that all students learn effective parenting skills prior to high school graduation. Further ensure that parents have good skills in mediating language.

<u>O</u> ptical and Auditory Systems

For students to benefit fully from school, it is essential that their optical/

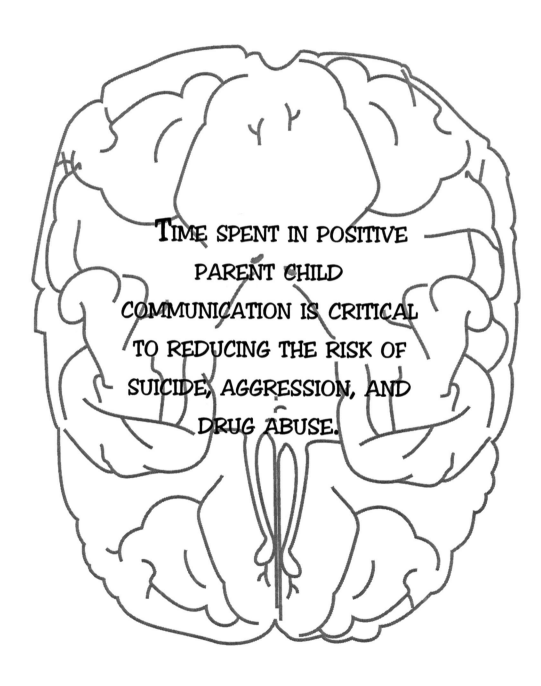

TIME SPENT IN POSITIVE PARENT CHILD COMMUNICATION IS CRITICAL TO REDUCING THE RISK OF SUICIDE, AGGRESSION, AND DRUG ABUSE.

visual and auditory systems be fully functioning. Difficulty in these areas is common with courageous learners. In author Donna's practice as a school psychologist, measures of auditory and/or visual *processing* were shown to be weak in approximately 80% of students referred for academic and behavioral difficulties.

Good medical check-ups are a must for school-aged youngsters. It is essential that their entire system be checked, including their vision and hearing. A medical check-up will reveal any difficulties with *acuity*. For example, during a visual examination we recently learned that author Donna's 7 year old nephew, Clancy, needed glasses for a small amount of nearsightedness.

Many of the approximately 80% of students referred to author Donna's school psychology practice for academic and/or behavioral difficulty who had trouble in the auditory and/or visual system(s), did not, however, have visual or auditory *acuity* problems. At least 70% of these students had *perceptual*, or *processing* difficulty in either the visual or auditory system, or both. Approximately 10% actually had *acuity* problems with one or both systems that were diagnosed medically.

Some studies have shown that 30% of school-aged children and youth have auditory processing problems. These difficulties can often be prevented if early ear infections are treated promptly so that they do not have a chance to limit important hearing of language in early childhood.

Programs such as *The Listening Program* by Advanced Brain Technologies are showing some promise for increasing listening skills, attention span, auditory perception, physical balance, focus, and more. This program is cited by the developers as being an auditory re-education program. It is based upon the study of the effect of special music and sound upon the human nervous system. The program consists of eight specially developed compact disks. Each disk contains four progressive segments that are 15 minutes each. The basic schedule calls for two 15 minute segments per day of headphone listening, 5 days a week, for a period of 8 weeks. (To contact the developers of this program go to www.advancedbrain.com.)

Promising research by Merzenich (1993) and Tallal (1994) indicates that a fast and simple program that uses computer games dramatically improves the speech skills of children with dyslexia and other language-based learning disabilities. The children engaged in the treatment enjoyed what they experienced as games as they rewired their brains so that they learned how to process speech sounds at a faster and more normal rate. (See reference list for

19

"I AM GOING TO BE THE BOSS OF MY BRAIN!" FROM A STUDENT AFTER LEARNING BrainSMART STRATEGIES.

STATE + STRATEGIES = SUCCESS

a complete citation on this research by Merzenich and Tallal that underlies the program *Fast Forward* or visit www.scientificlearning.com.)

Author Donna's diagnostic work in school psychology has indicated that a large number of individuals who are struggling with reading/writing activities are dealing with a visual *perception* dysfunction. She saw some of these students begin to succeed at reading and writing activities when they were diagnosed and treated for a difficulty called *Scotopic Sensitivity Syndrome* or *Irlen Syndrome* (1991). The syndrome is a perceptual dysfunction that causes varying degrees of print distortion and/or physical discomfort when the individual reads, especially black print on white paper. The perceptual dysfunction is caused by a particular sensitivity to certain color frequencies in full spectrum light. This light sensitivity can be diagnosed and treated using the Irlen Method. During the past 20 years, the scientific studies done on this learning difference have proven that the dysfunction is caused by full spectrum light, that each individual has their own particular frequencies that cause the difficulties, and that the Irlen Method of filtering the light provides an effective solution to the problem.

The Irlen Method (1991) is a researched process that modifies the light to each individual's precise need so that the distortions and discomforts associated with the syndrome do not occur. In our work we have seen some individuals benefit from Irlen lens in glasses to correct the perceptual dysfunction. In some cases schools have opted to screen for this difficulty and provide students with this syndrome with specially colored transparencies to be placed over printed material. This method helps students get clarity of visual perception so that they can begin to benefit from good reading instruction. For more information on this treatment for visual perceptual difficulty, contact the Irlen Institute at 1-562-496-2550, or for information about obtaining a screening contact Dr. Sally Church at 1-405-329-3852.

Other approaches such as the Ball-Stick-Bird reading series (Fuller, 1977) have been effective as methods used to teach students with problems in the area of visual perception. The Ball-Stick-Bird series derives its name from the way it teaches the alphabet: with Balls (circles), Sticks (lines), and Birds (angles) students make all the letters of the alphabet. The telling of stories, however, does not wait for the alphabet mastery. Space odysseys utilize principles from perceptual and developmental psychology in order to facilitate learning. As the letters of the alphabet are taught with only three symbols, there is less perceptual (visual) load for students to master who experience difficulty in this area.

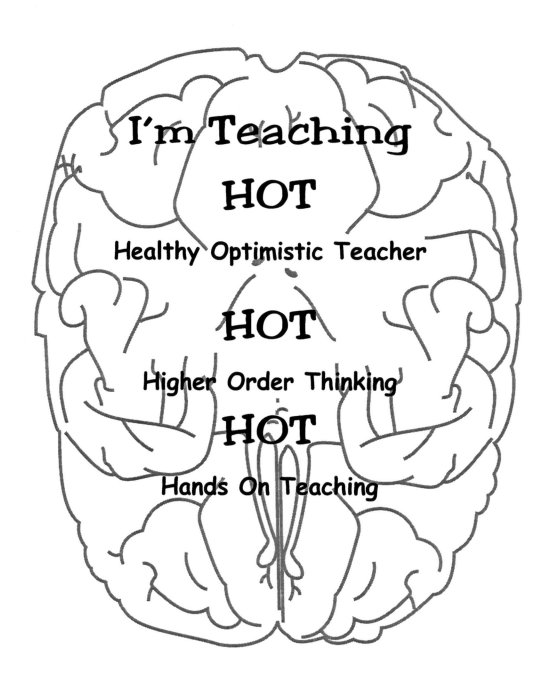

I'm Teaching

HOT

Healthy Optimistic Teacher

HOT

Higher Order Thinking

HOT

Hands On Teaching

U se it or Lose it

The brain is designed to lose it if it does not use it. Many courageous learners lack the kind of learning experiences they need to benefit from standard C.O.L.D teaching practice. Content Oriented Lecture and Ditto sheets. They are much more likely to learn from what we call HOT, HOT, HOT teaching. Healthy Optimistic Teachers, Hands On Teaching, and Higher Order Thinking.

Facts

- Students taught with hands on strategies were 70% ahead in science and 40% ahead in math.

- Repetitive use of ditto sheets without effective mediation by teachers does not improve student achievement and wastes precious learning time.

- Metacognition, thinking about thinking, is one of the most important factors in boosting student achievement.

Action

Ensure that you teach it HOT, HOT, HOT.

R ight hemispheric strengths

Many courageous learners have strong skills usually associated with right hemispheric brain function: seeing the big picture, rapid visual processing, and strong intuition. We can improve the probability of success when we bridge from these strengths.

Facts

- More than 75% of students at risk may have a right hemispheric strength.

- Students taught in their preferred learning style tend to learn more.

- Linear, fragmented, and abstract teaching styles are difficult to learn from.

Action

Teach students a toolbox of effective strategies for bridging from many

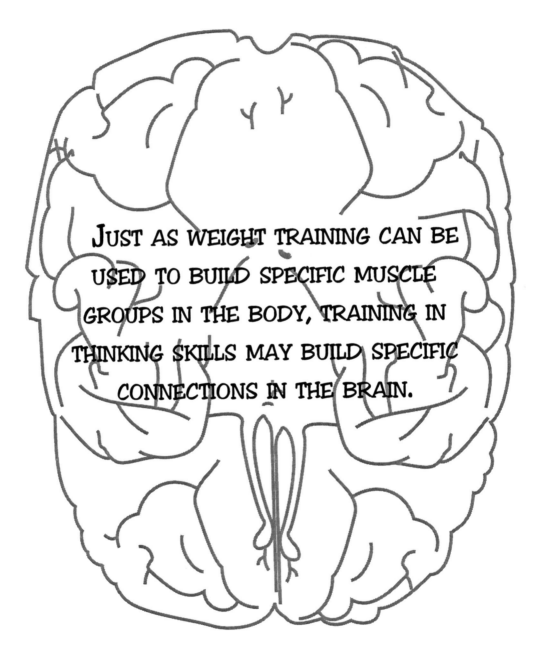

JUST AS WEIGHT TRAINING CAN BE USED TO BUILD SPECIFIC MUSCLE GROUPS IN THE BODY, TRAINING IN THINKING SKILLS MAY BUILD SPECIFIC CONNECTIONS IN THE BRAIN.

courageous learners strengths to academic success. The *BrainSMART Strategies for Boosting Test Scores* (2000) book has 60 strategies we have shared with 30,000 teachers for teaching students with these strengths.

A nalytical skills can be learned

The brain can be trained to change very specific functions. Research by Hiroshi Asanuma (as cited in Kotulak, 1996) found 25% more connections in the visual and kinesthetic areas of the brain after primates were taught how to catch objects.

In the case of humans, students today need to be able to analyze increasing amounts of information as schools and families keep up with the boon during the Information Age. In Chapter 4 we outline seven important thinking skills necessary for courageous learners to have a framework that will help them create successful lives. These seven skills were chosen because they are often skills that courageous learners have not learned when they arrive at school, and if not explicitly taught at school will cause these learners difficulty throughout school and life.

When we train teachers to use Feuerstein's (1980) program, Instrumental Enrichment, fully described in his book by the same name, they are equipped with the tools to teach over 50 important analytic strategies necessary for good thinking practice throughout life. *For more information on this program and when our next BrainSMART Thinking training* is offered, see us at www.brainsmart.com and contact author Donna at *donna@brainsmart.com* for more information.

G enes + environment + teaching = potential

One of the most exhilarating discoveries of the 20th century is that IQ is not fixed. Furthermore, it accounts for little of the lifetime success of an individual. The National Research Council (Bransford, Brown, & Cocking, 1999) estimates that IQ represents 4% of lifetime success. Others estimate around 10%.

E xpectations drive performance

Research suggests that teacher expectations have a profound impact on student achievement. At the same time many teachers of courageous learners have low expectations of their students based on past experience of the previous academic performance of such students. Breaking this negative cycle is imperative.

WE MUST ENSURE THAT
TEACHERS ARE GIVEN THE
TOOLS AND TRAINING THEY
NEED TO TEACH THE REAL
STUDENTS WHO ARRIVE IN
THEIR CLASSROOMS TODAY.
THE MYTHICAL MIDDLE CLASS,
WELL-BEHAVED STUDENTS OF
THE 1950s ARE NOT TURNING
UP ANYMORE.

Facts

- Teacher expectations drive student expectations and motivation.

- Teacher expectations change <u>after</u> they see their students' academic performance change.

- Teachers need to see peers producing good learning with similar students to their own.

Action

Ensure that teachers have excellent long term professional development that builds their capacity to facilitate success by courageous learners. Support the best teachers as master teachers who open their classroom doors to peers to encourage more effective teaching.

<u>O</u> ptions and choice improve motivation and learning.

Every brain is as unique as a fingerprint. Every student learns in their own way and at their own speed. When students have options in what they learn and how they learn it, the whole biology of the brain changes. One size fits all approaches are destined to fail many courageous learners. One teacher we worked with, named Beth Falter, gave her students a choice in how they demonstrated reading comprehension. They were allowed to either act out the story, draw it, or write it out, and reading comprehension went through the roof. As you will see in the "Barcode for the Brain" chapter, one of the parameters is Options or Procedures. As this example illustrates, courageous learners often respond well to having options available.

Facts

- The perception of options and choices boosts motivation.

- Teachers with the wide repertoire of teaching styles will tend to reach more learners more of the time.

- Providing options and choices will reduce the probability of classroom management issues.

Action

Work with your colleagues to find different ways for students to learn the same material. Make full use of cooperative learning settings and have small

We will need more than 2 million new teachers in the next decade. Imagine what would happen if they started their careers equipped with deep understanding of the science of learning and a practical system of instruction that maximizes their effectiveness as teachers.

groups working on a range of different approaches for solving the same problem.

U nderstanding

Courageous learners often bring great assets to the classroom in terms of courage, energy, and survival skills. If the school curriculum is designed with reality in mind so it connects with the real world of the students the school serves, the level of understanding will be high. If, however, the curriculum reflects a different world, understanding will be lower. For example, using a book about the beach when students have never been to one will be less meaningful than a story about the kind of neighborhood the students live in.

The temporal lobes of the brain are involved in the long term storage process. The more we can link to what is already in the temporal lobes, the higher the level of understanding will be. For example, often students who are good at street math, are unable to perform the same mathematical task in an abstract math lesson.

Facts

- Students who have had an adult to mediate meaning tend to learn how to create understanding in novel and unfamiliar settings.

- Meaningless data that is not used will often be deleted by the brain.

Action

We need to teach for meaning if we want gains in student achievement to occur.

S trategies

As we say at BrainSMART, State + Strategies = Success. For courageous learners to be successful they need to master healthy optimistic states and learn the thinking and learning strategies necessary for the task at hand. For example, SAT scores are best predicted by income level because it is suspected that higher income students get the inside track on how to beat the test. The greatest gift we can give courageous learners are the thinking, learning, and communication strategies that they need to benefit from the school experience for test taking and life.

Facts

- Students who have learned similar strategies produce similar results.

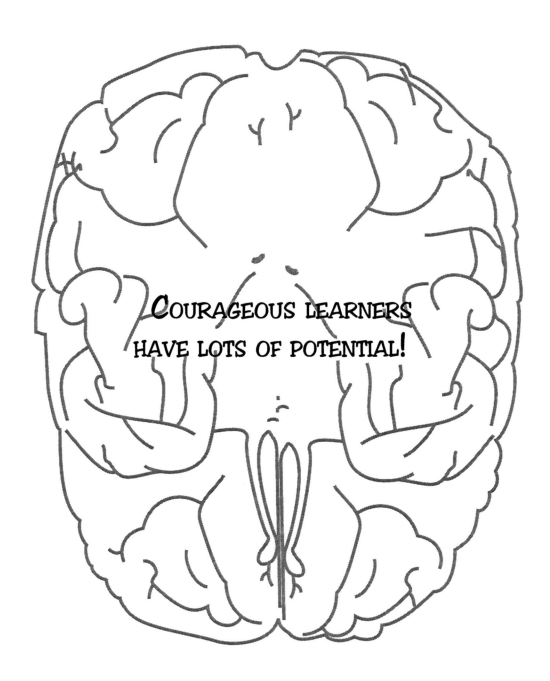

- Students are producing the best test scores that they can with the strategies that they have.

- Success with strategies produces a sense of efficacy that can translate to high motivation.

Action

Work with your colleagues to create High Five Strategy Time when you teach students a new strategy for thinking or learning and review for 5 minutes per day. After each session celebrate with a High Five. If your students learn one new strategy per week they will end up with 40 new strategies per year. (*"The Brain Guy" and "Dr. Donna" Top 40 Strategies Video Series is coming soon!*)

Chapter 2
Translating Research to Results

If the only tool you have is a hammer,
every problem looks like a nail.

Abraham Maslow

If the only tool you have is a hammer every problem looks like a nail.

If the last 50 years of research on effective teaching demonstrates one thing, it is that hammering away with tools that do not work is unlikely to result in increased student achievement. In fact, we argue that attempting to improve education by making tests harder without teaching the tools to allow students and teachers to be more successful is unlikely to yield the kind of results required at the present time. In Walberg's (1988) meta-analysis of 2,575 articles on improving student achievement, he came to the following conclusion. Mastery learning, acceleration programs, and reading training had large positive instructional effects. However, even though these methods have demonstrated positive effects in classroom research, they are not widespread practice.

Earlier research by Coleman and Jenks (as cited in Reynolds & Teddlie, 2000) suggested that school had minimal impact in academic success of students. In Goodlad's (1984) review of more than a thousand classrooms in America, he came to the conclusion that there had been little change in teaching practices in the recent years. Furthermore, research in the 1990's from the TIMSS study revealed that the countries with the highest mathematics scores in the world taught in a very different way from teachers in America. This study and others reported in the book, *The Teaching Gap,* by Stigler and Hiebert (1999), led the authors to reach the conclusion that the problem lies in methods of teaching and the absence of resources available to help teachers improve how they teach. Their work was based on observing videotapes from hundreds of classrooms in Japan, China, and America and noticing different instructional methodologies in these countries.

In our experience of working with more than 30,000 teachers we have come to the conclusion that the vast majority of teachers are committed to student success, and that they are open to exploring more effective ways to teach courageous learners in the classroom. Our mission is to support them in this effort. What is clear from reviews of the last fifty years of research and witnessing best practices first hand is as follows: 1) there are effective tools for teaching that can be learned by all teachers, 2) effective teaching will work with the vast majority of students, and 3) these practices can reconnect both teachers and learners to the joy of teaching and learning.

Different Brains, Different Learners

One of the exhilarating facts about educational research is that it is consistent in many findings. For example, leading educators and researchers

35

STATE

Helping students switch on positive,
low stress \ high challenge states

Great Teachers
Create Positive
and Optimistic
Learning States!

agree that standard teaching practice (lecture, worksheet, quiz) works well for a small minority of students. Hannaford (1995), Goodlad (1994), in *A Place Called School,* and Shanker (as cited in Healy, 1990) all agree that between fifteen to twenty percent of students do well with this mode of instruction. Hannaford (1995) describes this small group in her book *Smart Moves.* These students are linear and auditory processors that tend to look at the teacher. They are more likely to be left hemispheric dominant. So, the vast majority of today's students will not perform to their full potential when exposed to the standard system of instruction. In work by the National Association of Secondary School Principals, cited in David Sousa's (1995) book *How the Brain Learns,* the following facts were highlighted:

1) after twenty four hours of a traditional lecture, 95% of the information has been deleted (this fact is noted after only twenty four hours, so imagine the dramatic drop in recall weeks and months after the original lecture);

2) however, we notice that when students have a chance to discuss information retention rises to 50%;

3) when they use the information it rises to 75%; and,

4) when they teach someone else retention rises to 90%.

In our live BrainSMART workshops, we ensure that every participant experiences the above for themselves. First, we give them a number of words to remember. This is the pre-test. To avoid embarrassing the participants we do not ask them to reveal out loud how poorly they have done. Second, we teach a strategy for remembering all ten pieces of data. We then encourage them to discuss it with somebody else and teach each other the full list. Lastly, we do a post-test and virtually everybody has a 100% recall. The looks of joy on faces of participants at this point are phenomenal! This tool is usually transferred to the teachers' own children and students in the classroom within twenty-four hours. Great teachers of courageous learners in the classroom usually do use very different procedures for ensuring their students learn effectively.   They use stories, games, music, movement, and most importantly they make learning meaningful for the students by connecting it to the students' real world. Flanigan's research (as cited in Goodlad, 1984) with over 1,000 adults supports the effectiveness of creative teaching. Adults in his study were questioned about what they recalled from their high school education fifteen years earlier. The overwhelming response was, "very little." Lessons they did remember were the result of courageous teachers that had made learning meaningful and memorable.

In our combined fifty years of studying the brain and learning, we have yet

BrainSMART
Retention Probability Index

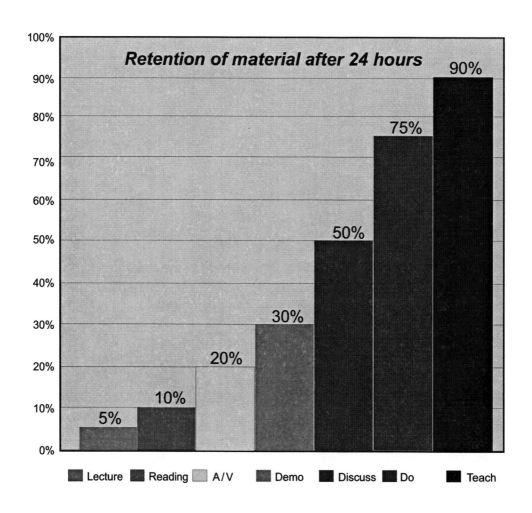

Adapted from Sousa, D. (1995).

www.brainsmart.com

to find substantial data that supports the standard system of instruction. Therefore, it is by systematically changing the instruction that we will change the level of student achievement that occurs in our schools.

Deming is Right: The Ninety Four/Six Phenomenon

When working in Japan to launch a British airline, author Marcus was amazed at the Japanese philosophy of continuous self-improvement. In business it was described as Kaizen and the literal translation is "change good". What impressed Marcus even more was the dramatic improvement in the quality of Japanese products. Deming (1994), America's leading statistician, learned from over sixty years of experience that 94% of results are produced by the system and 6% by special causes. Others in the quality movement have refined this to be 85% produced by the system and 15% by special causes.

The key point is that the current level of academic achievement by at risk-learners is being produced by the current system. If we want to change the results, we need to change the system. The need to do this is dramatically amplified by the fact that the system of support many students receive from parents and community in their early years, and, in fact, throughout their school lives has changed dramatically.

The System of the Home

Research suggests that many students, particularly those that we define as courageous learners, are receiving less support for their intellectual, emotional, and psychological growth than ever before. *A USA Today* study (as cited in Amen, 1998) revealed that the average parent spends less than seven minutes a week in dialogue with their child. The Carnegie report (as cited in Education Commission of the States, 1997) highlighted the fact parents now spend 30% less time with their children. Kotulak's book, *Inside the Brain*, highlights the fact that the average student from a welfare family has had thirteen million words less of language exposure than their counterparts. The net result is that by age four, children from such a background have about half the working vocabulary as other children. This is happening at a time when the average American family is earning less then they were twenty years ago and many parents are having to work longer hours. With an epidemic of depression and pessimism sweeping the country, many parents are unable to provide the support system that children need. Furthermore, approximately 50% of students will live in a single parent family by the time they are 18 years of age.

What must be made clear, however, is that the socioeconomic status of the

BrainSMART

94% of results are produced by the system
6% by special causes

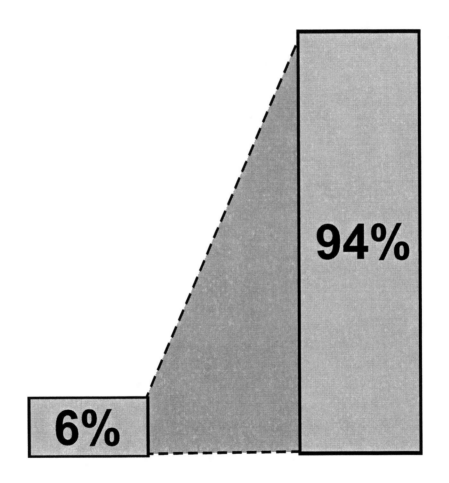

Adapted from Deming, W. (1994).

www.brainsmart.com

family is not the primary determinant of the child's success at school. Walberg (1988) asserts that the curriculum of the home is twice as important in predicting academic learning as is socioeconomic status. His definition of curriculum of the home is a system of talking about daily events. For example, such things as monitoring, watching, and discussing television together and dining together.

Another component critical to the health and success of courageous learners is the diet and exercise habits learned from home. For example, the average American consumed around 150 pounds of sugar in 1996 (as cited in Peskin & Conyers, 2000). This is a dramatic increase in sugar consumption that is continuing. Now the average child weighs ten pounds more then they did eight years ago and obesity and overweight status among children is growing in epidemic proportions with incidents of diabetes on the rise.

With these factors systematically shaping the courageous learner's brain and body system, it is even more critical that the school be organized to allow them to be successful when they are at school.

Pareto Power: The 20/80 Solution

Courageous learners achieve academic success when they receive high intensity and effective instruction. Such students start school with fewer positive learning experiences than the general population. They therefore need more educational experiences to catch up. Effective teachers focus their energy on the 20% of teaching practice that produces 80% of the learning results. For example "hands on" teaching can often produce more learning than the handing out of ditto sheets. The 20/80 rule (Koch, 1998) was originated by Vilfredo Pareto, an Italian economist who noted that 20% of the population owned 80% of the wealth. This relationship can be seen in many other contexts. For example 20% of students will tend to produce 80% of the classroom management issues. When teachers focus on creating powerful and engaging learning experiences, 80% of classroom management issues are solved. We have enormous admiration for the great work that the educators of students at-risk do. In our workshops we encourage teachers to focus on the "20 that gets 80" (Koch, 1998). This principle is a powerful one for the whole educational team to learn. Imagine what would happen if curriculum developers were trained to focus on the 20% of curriculum that produces 80% of understanding, and if teachers were trained to use the 20% of classroom teaching approaches that produced 80% of the learning.

BrainSMART
20% of Actions produce 80% of Results

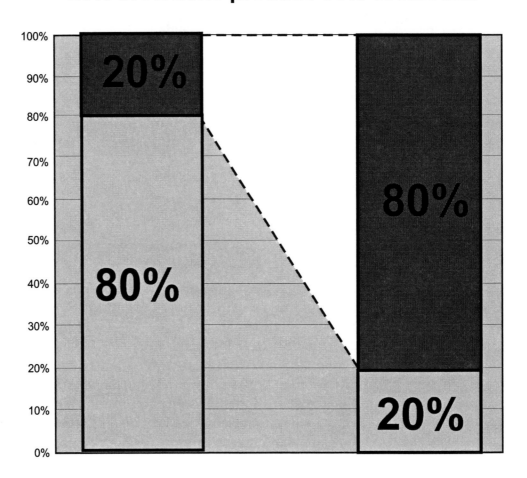

Adapted from Koch, R. (1998).

www.brainsmart.com

The Children Are Different Today

One of the highlights of our work at BrainSMART is that we get the opportunity to visit many classrooms at all grade levels to see what great teachers are doing and how courageous learns are contributing to their own success. One of the most dramatic changes that we have noticed is the rapid increase in the number of students who exhibit the symptoms of being more right hemispheric dominant and kinesthetic in learning style. In working with 30,000 teachers in many workshops, we ask participants what style of student they are seeing in their classroom. The overwhelming response is that they are also seeing more right brained, kinesthetic learners, and that this is putting a strain on their ability to teach effectively.

Again drawing from Dr. Carla Hannaford's (1995) book *Smart Moves* we see an analysis that illustrates this change. Her research indicates that approximately 80% of students in special education are more right brained dominant (gestalt), and that around 80% of students in the gifted programs are more left hemispheric dominant (logic). These more left hemispheric dominant students are the very ones that will tend to do well in a system that teaches and tests a narrow range of student abilities, namely verbal and mathematical intelligence. Harvard's Dr. Howard Gardner (1983) has identified at least 8 or 9 intelligences. The two intelligences that we usually teach, verbal linguistic and logical mathematical, are a fraction of the limitless potential of a human being.

The challenge facing educators of courageous learners is that the traditional system of teaching that works ineffectively with the majority of students, will be even less effective with particular styles of learning. Furthermore, if we begin to increase the pressure on students to succeed at scoring well on standardized tests and use an increased number of ditto sheets for instruction, we are likely to increase the failure and frustration level of many students.

Research (Hannaford, 1995) indicates that under stress more right hemispheric dominant students experience a reaction that is different from many other people. First, they have difficulty taking in sensory data, and then withdraw. They process with internal images and are unable to explain what is happening verbally. More importantly, they need to move. Imagine what happens in a classroom where a stressed out teacher sincerely wants the students to succeed, demands that they explain how they came to conclusion verbally, and insist that they sit still. The teachers that we work with are certain that these situations are more and more common. In short, the more right hemispheric kinesthetic system of teaching that many courageous learners need to be successful is seldom experienced in U.S. classrooms. We

BrainSMART
Logic / Gestalt Brain Style Types

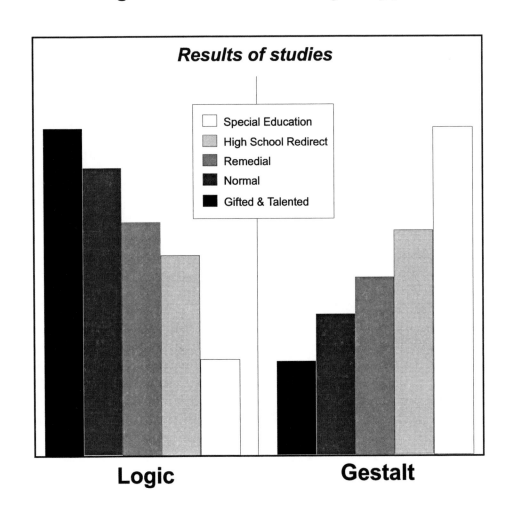

Adapted from Hannaford, C. (1995).

www.brainsmart.com

have seen students show immediate and dramatic improvement in their learning when they are taught using what we call BrainSMART strategies.

In effect, our philosophy is to build a bridge from the strength that courageous learners bring. They are often very good at visualizing, using kinesthetic strategies for learning, and for creative processing. The other part of the process to insure that courageous learners become successful is that we need to strengthen students' ability to use left hemispheric skills such as planning, impulse control, and time and space management. Author Donna will address these specifically in the thinking skills chapter.

Show Me the Money

One of the reasons that we are so proud to live in America is that it is the birthplace of democracy. We are still inspired by the constitution installing liberty and justice for all. One of the most exciting factors about research on the brain and cognition is that we now have a roadmap to move towards this national mission in a practical way in our schools.

The financial implications of this are enormous, as is the social justice issue. For example, it is estimated that every two students who drop out of school cost the community 1.5 million dollars (as cited in Washington & Andrews, 1998). Furthermore, every year's worth of students dropping out costs 90 billion dollars in lifetime revenue and contributions. We believe that businesses, communities, and schools must align around the mission of equipping every student with the thinking, learning, and communicating tools they need to be successful in school and in life. It just makes sense.

A great example of this alignment occurred in Orlando, Florida. Authors Donna and Marcus "The Brain Guy" had the privilege of working with Communities in Schools in partnership with Prudential. Marcus provided a keynote to some 750 adolescent leaders who had been through an extensive leadership program. These high school students were some of the most courageous learners that we have ever met. In order to communicate the importance of education, Marcus showed an overhead which highlights the impact of getting an education in America. He made it clear that if you decide to drop out of school it will cost you a half a million dollars in lifetime income. However, if you can graduate from high school and go on to get a college degree your lifetime income can go up to 3.4 million dollars. There was a hush in the room as the students began to think about what had been said. Marcus then asked the organizers of this conference if he could have 20 minutes of question time with this group. He knew from previous experience that the students would ask excellent questions. The students came up to the microphone, one by one, to ask some of the best questions we have ever

Under Stress

Right Hemispheric and Usually Gestalt Learners

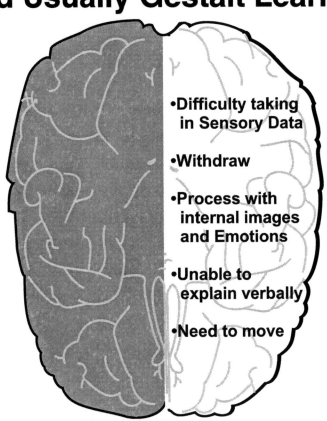

- Difficulty taking in Sensory Data
- Withdraw
- Process with internal images and Emotions
- Unable to explain verbally
- Need to move

Adapted from Hannaford, C. (1997).

www.brainsmart.com

heard. Such is the awesome power of courageous learners to come through time and time again.

What was heartbreaking about the conference was that many students would not be graduating from high school because they had failed to pass mathematics. The reason the students were not successful in mathematics was due to a large extent to students and teachers not being given the tools and the time to learn mathematics effectively. This event moved Marcus to make learning mathematics a priority in terms of our work in equipping all students with the tools of success. (Authors Marcus and Donna will be publishing two new guidebooks called *Health Math* and *Wealth Math* in 2001 with ways to make mathematics meaningful, memorable, and learnable).

Inspired by this leadership conference, Marcus and Donna went on to explore what percentage of students from lower income went on to get a bachelors degree. The answer is tragic. In research by Rendon, Hope, and Associates (cited in Kaplan & Edelfelt, 1996) suggest that approximately 4% of low-income students complete their bachelor's degree. This compares with the graduation of 76% of high-income families. At a time when the economy desperately needs a large supply of well educated graduates, there is obviously a tremendous opportunity to boost the economy by transforming potential high school drop outs into high performing graduates. For example, in Los Angeles County, it is estimated that in the year 2015 the country will require 200,000 more college graduates than the supply will deliver. At the same time, they will have 175,000 high school dropouts who will be having a difficult time finding a job (as cited in Washington & Andrews, 1998). Imagine then the financial impact of equipping students with the tools they need to be successful through high school right through to college graduation. Of course, getting into a good college requires high S.A.T. scores and the competition is fierce. In Alfie Kohn's (1999) excellent book, *The Schools Our Children Deserve*, he highlights the fact that high income rather than superior intellect predicts S.A.T scores.

One of the reasons that high-income students tend to get higher S.A.T scores is that they often get the test taking skills that lower income students seldom receive.

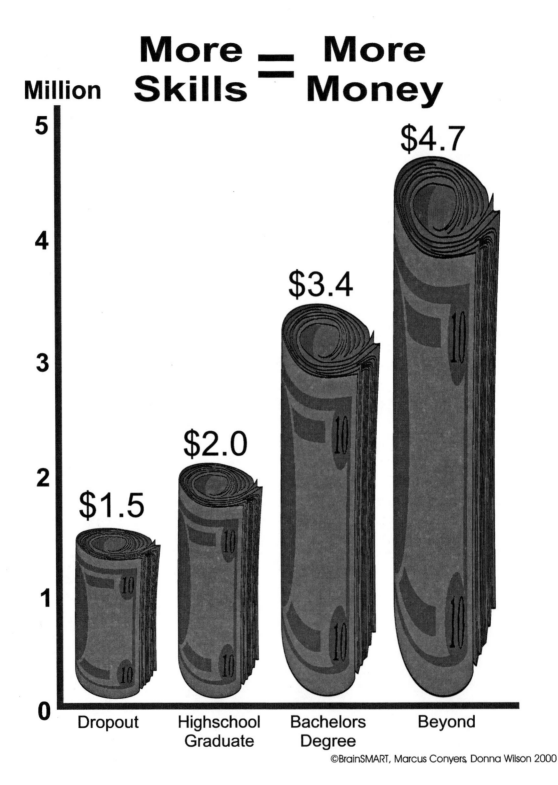

More Skills = More Money

©BrainSMART, Marcus Conyers, Donna Wilson 2000

College Admission Test Scores by Family Income 1998

INCOME	SCORE
Less than $10,000	873
$10,000 - $20,000	918
$20,000 - $30,000	972
$30,000 - $40,000	993
$40,000 - $50,000	1015
$50,000 - $60,000	1033
$60,000 - $70,000	1048
$70,000 - $80,000	1062
$80,000 - $100,000	1084
Above $100,000	1130

Summary of Chapter 2: We have reached a historic moment in the history of education. There is an opportunity to translate research into real world results starting right now. Our review of the last 50 years of educational research around the world, and our own work with more than 30,000 educators, have guided us to the following conclusions about what we need to do to allow courageous learners to unleash their true potential.

Fact One: Standard teaching practice, as experienced by many of the 50 million students in America today, with the best efforts of hard working teachers, is unlikely to result in significant gains in student achievement.

Fact Two: Across America, and around the world, creative and innovative teachers have always moved beyond standard practice to teach in ways that naturally engage the human brain. The explosion in neuroscience is finally able to begin to explain why these approaches are so successful.

Fact Three: The use of systematic, research based, best practices will dramatically increase the potential for students at-risk to become successful. It is certain that teachers can learn these best practices. By creating learning communities within their schools and districts, they can transform best practices into powerful lessons that can be shared and consistently used throughout their schools for positive effect on student achievement. The

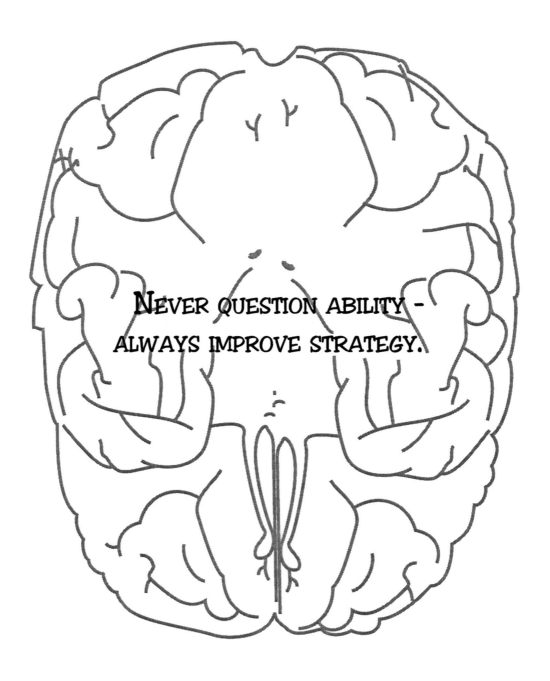

NEVER QUESTION ABILITY –
ALWAYS IMPROVE STRATEGY.

National Staff Development Council, in their work to promote excellent professional development, confirms the fact that equipping teachers with the time that they need to learn these practices is critical if student achievement gains are to be achieved. Rand Corporation also confirms this finding with the discovery that most teachers require 50 hours of practice to initiate new teaching processes (as cited in *The National Education Commission of Time and Learning*, April 1994). The late Albert Shanker also highlighted this when he commented on the fact new processes to build cars that workers were equipped with 92 hours of training to allow them to do their part (as cited in Stigler & Hiebert, 1999). Surely teachers, in their role as practitioners of neuroscience for boosting achievement, are worthy of at least this amount of time!

Fact Four: Many courageous learners are not likely to be receiving the support from their home life that they need to be successful in school. This is especially true in terms of acquiring the thinking, learning, and communicating skills they need to benefit from current teaching practice. Research shows that students can learn these tools when taught in the right way. When these skills are taught the benefit to students, teachers, and parents alike is profound. Students can increase their impulse control, manage space and time more effectively, stay focused on their lessons, problem solve more effectively, and make better decisions when they have been taught the skills for doing so. They can choose which learning tools they need in each situation and may ask themselves the question, "How am I going to learn this?"

Since 94% of results are produced by the system and 6% by special causes, it is clear that it is the system of instruction and the system of teaching students to learn how to learn that must be changed, if we wish to achieve positive results. Simply making tasks harder and holding teachers accountable for doing what they have not been taught how to do and not giving them the time to do it, is likely to be unsuccessful.

Changing the system requires the kind of courageous leadership that we have seen over and over again by those who gain courage from being equipped with the right information and learning that the "good stuff" works from their own life experiences. In the next chapter we will explore the "Four Fundamental Forces for driving student achievement. Here we will address the specific areas that have the highest impact on the success of courageous learners in our classrooms and beyond.

Chapter 3
Four
Fundamental
Forces
of Learning

The Learning Forces Model for Boosting Student Achievement

Force 1: Professional Development and Teacher Preparation

Force 2: Physical/Mental Health and Safety

Force 3: Parent Support, Mentors, and Peers

Force 4: Pre K, Pre Natal, and Prior Knowledge

Introduction: The 4-Forces Model

"A system is a network of interdependent components that work together to try to achieve the aim of the system."

W. Edwards Deming
In *The New Economics* (1994)

"If I were a young scientist today, I would still do immunization. But instead of immunizing kids physically, I'd do it your way. I'd immunize them psychologically. I'd see if these psychologically immunized kids could then fight off mental illness better and physical illness, too."

Jonas Salk, M.D.
Nobel Laureate speaks to
Martin Seligman as reported
in *The Optimistic Child* (1995)

We stand today at a point in history where we know more about what it takes to equip courageous learners with the tools to become successful citizens of the 21st Century. As Deming confirms, what is required to make the transformation between potential and results, is a well synchronized system of support to unleash the brain power of students from at-risk situations.

An effective system will work on two levels. First, as Nobel Laureate, Jonas Salk, advocates in *The Optimistic Child* (Seligman, 1995), a process for immunizing courageous learners against the risk factors that increase their probability of failure is necessary. Secondly, at the intervention level, schools need to equip all the adult participants in the system with the tools for remediating students who have not had the learning experiences necessary to be successful. As our friend and colleague, Dr. Reuven Feuerstein (1980), eloquently states, "It is not a matter of learning traits, but learning states." His seminal work comes from teaching adolescent and young adult victims of the Holocaust how to open themselves to powerful learning again after great loss in their lives.

From our review of the last 50 years of research on increasing student achievement, we have identified what we term, "The Four Learning Forces," that drive the success, or failure, of students in the system. By harnessing these forces, we can maximize positive academic gain by courageous learners, and minimize the cost within the system.

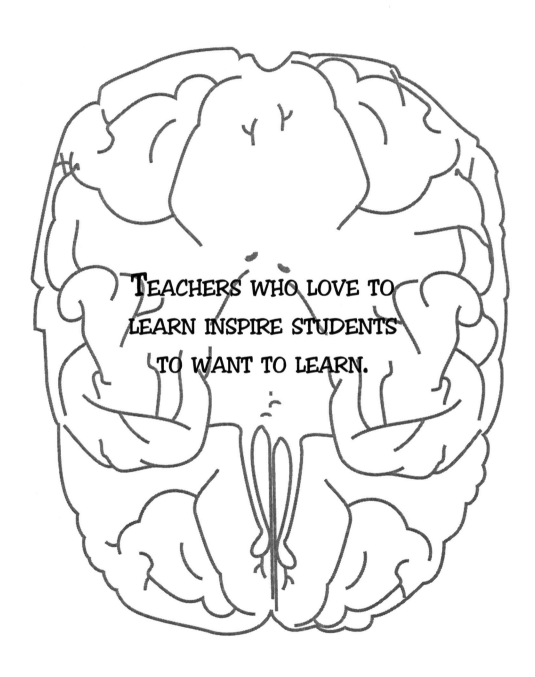

TEACHERS WHO LOVE TO
LEARN INSPIRE STUDENTS
TO WANT TO LEARN.

Force 1: Professional Development and Teacher Preparation

What Works -

High student achievement is the direct result of having a succession of competent, caring, and well-trained teachers

What is happening -

- 4 in 5 teachers do not feel capable of teaching students today

- 75% of teachers in the classroom in the year 2000 were not in the classroom in 1990

- 40% drop out of teaching in the first 5 years

- 40% students are in an at-risk situation at school

- Chronic shortage of teachers in math, science, and special education

Solutions -

- Recruit, retain, and equip teachers with the attitudes, skills, and knowledge they need to raise student achievement

- Utilize research based rapid positive impact solutions in the classroom

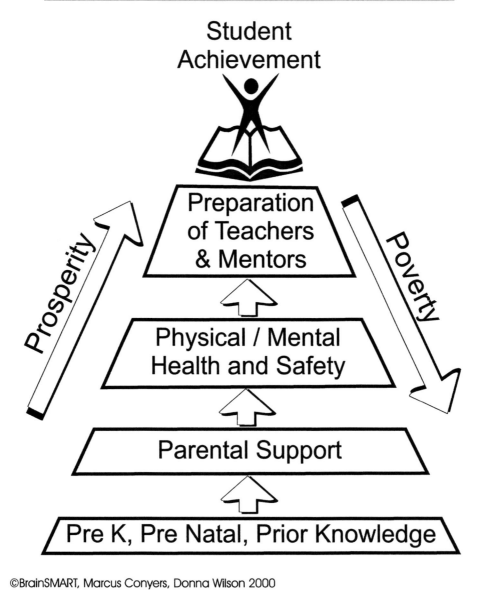

Four Learning Forces That Drive Student Achievement

Student Achievement

Preparation of Teachers & Mentors

Prosperity

Poverty

Physical / Mental Health and Safety

Parental Support

Pre K, Pre Natal, Prior Knowledge

©BrainSMART, Marcus Conyers, Donna Wilson 2000

In author Donna's experience as a school psychologist, she was a team member who worked to move student achievement forward by encouraging community stakeholders to speak the same language when creating programs for courageous learners. The team consisted of educators: regular and special education teachers, counselors, school psychologists, administrators, parents, and paraprofessionals. These stakeholders met to coordinate services for courageous learners in Norman, Oklahoma (Wilson & Church, 1993). (This story is further articulated in Chapter 7.)

Force 1: Professional Development and Teacher Preparation

Duttweiler and Robinson (1999) cite William Saunders, Ph.D., who confirms that a significant increase in student achievement by previously low achieving students was possible when taught by highly effective teachers. The increase in achievement was as high as 53%, in contrast to a maximum of a 14% increase by students taught by a less effective teacher. Saunders concluded that this could potentially determine the difference between a remedial label vs. placement on a gifted track.

Currently, 4 out of 5 teachers report that they do not feel capable of teaching effectively in today's classrooms (as cited in Duttweiler & Robinson, fall 1999). Furthermore, although long-term professional development significantly improves teacher effectiveness, only 15% of teachers are supported in this way.

Force 2: Physical/Mental Health and Safety

In order for courageous learners to be successful in school and life, it is vital that they sustain peak physical, mental, and emotional health. First, we will give some important facts about physical health in the U.S.

Physical Health

We are in the grips of an epidemic of obesity as never seen before. The average student today is around 8 pounds heavier than they were just 10 years ago. There are two primary reasons for this to be happening. People are exercising less than ever before. Research suggests that few students are getting the 30 minutes of exercise every day that is necessary to maintain health and maximize protection against illness. Furthermore, many schools are actually cutting back the amount of time available for sports and physical exercise. The likely physical effect of insufficient exercise is an increase in depression, stress, and aggression, as well as obesity. Research on student

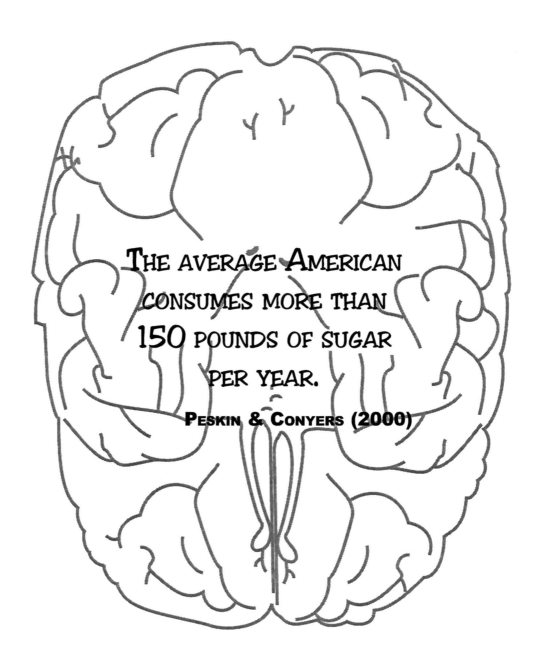

THE AVERAGE AMERICAN CONSUMES MORE THAN 150 POUNDS OF SUGAR PER YEAR.

PESKIN & CONYERS (2000)

Force 2: Physical/ Mental Health and Safety Facts

- Childhood depression is now at 23%.

- Depression is now the 4th leading cause of disease in the U.S.

- In 2020 it will be the leading cause of disease in the U.S.

- Incidents of suicide and violence are increasing and at lower ages.

- 50% of U.S. citizens are overweight.

- 75 –90% of visits to the doctor are stress related.

- Solutions:

- Teach Children How to Exercise

- Teach Children to Eat Nutritious Meals

- Train Children to be More Optimistic

Force 3: Parent Support, Mentors, and Peers

- **Facts:**

  The average parent spends less than 7 minutes per week talking with their children.

  Only one young child in two is read to every day.

- **Solutions:**

  Engage your children in dialogue.

  Read to your children every day.

achievement in mathematics from Japan shows that students who exercised regularly seemed calmer, more focused, and less disruptive.

The second major cause of obesity and overweight status is poor nutrition. Ponder the following question. If you knew that there was a cost effective way to improve student test scores simply by changing what students eat, what would you do? You might say, "Let's do it!" Consider the following research. A four year study in New York City Public Schools demonstrated an increase in student achievement by reducing sucrose and additives served in school lunches (as cited in Peskin & Conyers, 2000). The research was conducted with 1 million students in 803 schools across the city, and achievement gains were seen in the students' grades from a pre intervention average of 11% below to 5% above on national means. School districts that are genuinely committed to improving student achievement and test scores have a great opportunity to do so, while increasing the health of students in their communities.

There has been a dramatic increase in the consumption of sugar (Peskin & Conyers, 2000) in the U.S. In the late 1700s consumption was 4 pounds per person per year. In 1996, sugar consumption increased to 150 pounds per person per year. These unnecessary and empty calories are a major contributor to the obesity challenge. Furthermore, many students find it difficult to concentrate after high sugar consumption. For verification of this fact, ask any teacher of courageous learners. Additionally, many students are deficient in essential fatty acids. Supplements have been shown to reduce depression and symptoms of hyperactivity and other attention problems.

One of the greatest opportunities for increasing academic achievement by courageous learners is to ensure that they have the exercise and nutrition they need to support the brain body system. The physical health of students might be considered as support for the hardware of learning. Every dollar and minute invested here will have an immediate and positive impact and will help the U.S. avoid massive costs in the future.

Mental and Emotional Health

One of the greatest predictors of the academic success of courageous learners is the development of healthy optimistic thinking. This may be considered the software for learning. Research by Dr. Martin Seligman (1995), with more than 400,000 people over 25 years, has confirmed that optimism, or pessimism and helplessness, are learned.

Many courageous learners come from situations that support a pessimistic outlook. The exciting news is that when such students are taught how to think optimistically, they have a much greater chance of academic and life success. Such teaching is critical at a time when 23% of students

Force 4: Pre-K and Pre-Natal

- **Facts**

Only two in every three children start school ready to learn.

The caregiver – child relationship is critical for relating and learning.

Early childhood interventions can reduce the numbers of students needing special education by 50%.

Every nine children prevented from entering special education saves one million dollars.

Only five percent of students who enter special education return to the regular classroom annually. One-third drop out, and 1.5% get a diploma.

Effective interventions can boost intelligence quotients (IQs) by 10 to 20 points and cut the risk of mental retardation by 50%.

experience depression, and some researchers, such as Sapolsky, indicate that100% of people in the U.S. are likely to experience stress. Stress, pessimism, and depression are often precursors to violent behavior. So, as practical optimism is learned, the incidence of violence will likely decrease.

Force 3: Parent and Mentor Support

Courageous learners spend, at most, 13% of their waking hours in school during the first 18 years of life. The other 87% of time is spent in the family and larger community. Research has confirmed that while socioeconomic status is a factor in determining student achievement, it is overshadowed by the fabulous opportunity for parents and mentors to make a difference in young lives. For example, what researcher Walberg (1998) described as the "curriculum of the home" has twice as much impact on student achievement as the family's socioeconomic status.

When mediation, or guiding, is done well, it can have as much as a ten-fold greater impact than economic factors. For example, authors Donna and Marcus have keynoted conferences for Parent Educators with the Texas Association of School Boards, Parent Learning Network and have seen very positive results of good parent and mentor education.

Force 4: Pre K and Pre Natal

The explosion of research on the plasticity of the human brain, from conception through age 4, is a double-edged sword. On the one hand, a positive, nurturing, and stimulating environment can build the foundation for lifelong academic and social success. On the other hand, absence of such support can result in increased risk of failure. For example, the simple act of regular dialogue with young children has an enormous impact.

By the time they are 4 years old, children in white-collar families have experienced around 13,000,000 more words than children in welfare families (as cited in Conyers & Heverly, 1999). The net result of this fact is that children from welfare families start school with 50% of the vocabulary of children from white-collar families. Further, the research also shows that when parents read to children, it has a strong positive impact on literacy skills. However, in the U.S., 30 to 50% of children are not read to everyday. We now have an exciting opportunity to encourage these two important activities that do have a profound and long lasting impact on children's later success at school. Talking and reading to young children everyday in a positive and caring manner will make a great difference later in the area of academic achievement.

65

Chapter 4
BrainSMART Tools for Thinking

67

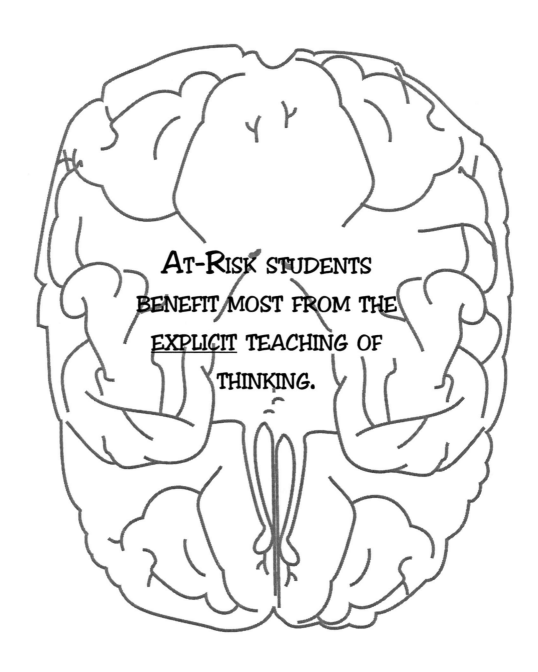

At-Risk students benefit most from the EXPLICIT teaching of thinking.

At-Risk Learners and Thinking
Research for Better Schools Defines Important Issues

☛ The system promotes the belief that these students can not learn and think well.

☛ Standards tend to be set too low.

☛ Systems need to be structured to assess potential, not just measure deficits.

☛ Professional development and teacher education programs need to equip teachers with understanding and skills about learning potential and cognitive instruction.

☛ Students need to have access to <u>t</u>hinking and <u>l</u>earning <u>c</u>oaches - TLCs.

☛ Systems need to be structured for at-risk learners to have access to instruction for acquiring higher order thinking, not just basic skills.

☛ School governing boards need to seriously consider the policies affecting at-risk students.

Adapted from Presseisen, 1988

When we ask groups of educators who gets the best instruction in thinking, they tell us "the gifted students." Those who need it most do not receive needed instruction in thinking.

Why Courageous Learners Need Thinking Skills

As a component of her doctoral studies, author Donna examined the literature on at-risk students and the teaching of thinking. She found that in the Philadelphia based offices of *Research for Better Schools*, Presseisen (1988) interrelated the research from these two areas and suggests four major issues of concern for education regarding at-risk learners.

The **first** issue is the pervasive doubt in U.S. school systems that at-risk learners can be successful. Members of the education community believe these learners are not capable of learning like other students or that they can learn how to think. Therefore, programs for these students may have lowered standards. Additionally, as Hilliard (1987) points out, evaluation instruments, such as the Learning Potential Assessment Device (that assesses potential for learning rather than only measuring deficits) need to be used with this population. Most importantly, professional development programs and teacher education programs need to develop concepts about learning potential and cognitive instruction, so that educators will be empowered to help at-risk learners transform their lives.

The **second** issue is the role of the teacher in classroom instruction, particularly with at-risk learners. Presseisen (1988) draws upon the work of other educational leaders who emphasize the role of the teacher as mediator, or classroom coach, gentle questioner, high motivator, and steady guide. Conceptualizing the teacher as mediator/coach appears to address others' concerns regarding disengaged learners. The idea of the teacher as mediator/coach also addresses the issues of minority culture participation through language.

Through interaction with the classroom mediator/coach, as well as through active participation with peers in learning in the classroom, valuable information from the students' minority culture will become a part of the life and dialogue in the classroom. Active learning of minority cultures represented in a classroom would then be possible. The classroom would be a "safe place" for these students to share while being guided by a mediator/coach who values all students' cultural heritage and is explicitly trained to express this value.

A **third** concern is a need for emphasis on high-order thinking and not just basic skills. If the at-risk students remain in remedial programs that only address basic skills, they will forever remain dependent learners. Leaders in business and labor report great concern that many employees are unable to have successful lives of work due to an inability to problem solve in the workplace.

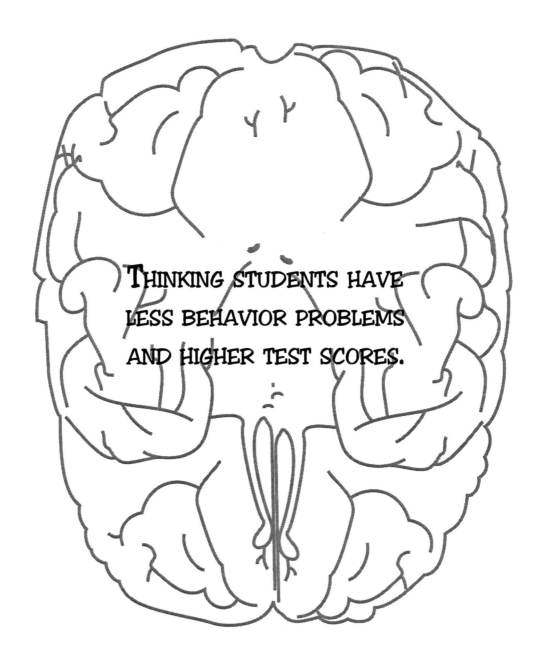

THINKING STUDENTS HAVE
LESS BEHAVIOR PROBLEMS
AND HIGHER TEST SCORES.

Courageous Learners Become Better Thinkers

Here's How!

- Teach thinking apart from content. At-risk students are often behind in their learning of content. If we intervene with content instruction only, they become increasingly more frustrated. However, when explicitly taught learning and thinking tools, they can begin to catch up with peers on a more level playing field.

- Explicit instruction and labeling of thinking strategies leads to greater metacognition. Students begin to be able to examine their own thinking process. This is very important for success in life and on high-stakes standardized testing practices today.

Four Factors for Boosting Student Achievement

1. Use metacognition

2. Use cognitive strategies

3. Have teacher that is interested in relating with them

4. Access instruction that includes their style learning

Adapted from
Research by Wang,
Haertel, and Walberg
(1993)

Finally, Presseisen (1988) considers the policymaking aspect of teaching at-risk students to be more effective thinkers. She poses the following questions: What impact do grouping practices have on the development of at-risk students thinking skills? How important is it that schools have a positive climate that encourages collegial contact for both teachers and students? How long should the school year be for these learners to receive the maximum benefit of their education?

Courageous Learners Can Become Better Thinkers

Researcher Adams (1989) has examined the importance of teaching thinking to at-risk learners. In an examination of the literature on thinking and this group of students, she found that they have needs significantly different from learners who are not at-risk in U.S. schools.

The first is that at-risk students need to be taught effective thinking strategies apart from content. After thinking strategies are taught, they may then be connected to academic content and life experiences through classroom dialogue around meaningful curriculum and life. It is a boon for these students to not be punished immediately for the fact that often they come into our classrooms content poor. With an initial focus on thinking principles, the at-risk students are on an equal playing field with other students, rather than at a disadvantage. Then, as they learn content as it is presented through engaging methods, students apply thinking principles to academic content.

Second, the explicit instruction and labeling of thinking strategies leads to greater metacognition. Metacognition can be defined as thinking about one's own thinking. An example of the use of the ability to think about one's own thinking is that students become better able to discuss their own process of problem solving and to be aware or what they know and what they do not know. Not only is this skill important on a daily basis in life and school, it is now extremely valuable in high stakes testing in state examinations where explaining the thinking process is critical for obtaining high scores.

In a very important 91 study meta-analysis of predictors of high student achievement, researchers at the University of Chicago (Wang, Haertel, & Walberg, 1993) have reported that the most important student characteristic for high student achievement is metacognition. The good news for at-risk learners is that this is a teachable skill. The meta-analysis also revealed two other important criteria for developing high achievers in our schools. In addition to metacognition, it is important for students to learn strategies for thinking in relationship with a teacher who cares for them.

Awareness of Growth

Aware

www.brainsmart.com

Courageous Learners
Become Better Thinkers In
Relationship with A
Coach for Thinking

Characteristics of "Coach Thinking"

- It is practical and optimistic.

- The intent is to teach students the 20% that gets 80% of the results.

- Teacher is learner as well as teacher.

- Both teacher and students question themselves as part of the learning process.

- The teacher models questioning aloud so that students become metacognitive – that is they think about their own learning.

- Thinking and learning for school and life is front and center in the classroom.

- The school supports teachers with adequate resources for implementation.

3 Major Principles for Creating Thinking Classrooms

The classroom is set up for maximum joyful interaction between the teacher and students & students together

Thinking and learning for school and life is front and center in the classroom.

The system provides necessary support for teachers and students to learn new ways to think and learn.

Relating for Learning: The Teacher – Student Relationship

In our workshops across the U.S. and internationally, we feel fortunate to have experienced first-hand the stories of teachers who have impacted the lives of their students. These courageous teachers invest time into understanding the strategies that will help their students become more successful. It is a joy to hear their stories of hope engendered through the use of successful methods that have worked with courageous learners!

A compelling story that we often remember when confronted with a challenge is one fraught with optimism and difficulty. It is a story born out of the Holocaust and provides an understanding about the power of the teacher and student relationship in learning. Dr. Reuven Feuerstein (1980), developer of the theory and practice of mediated learning, worked with adolescents and young adults who survived the Holocaust, but had suffered great loss. Many of those that Feuerstein worked with had lost their family to death and, in fact, rarely even had photographs from their past.

Through a caring relationship as their teacher, Feuerstein's (1980) spirit of practical optimism lifted survivors so that they could rise and see the new day. As time went on, he guided them to become optimistic about contributing to culture through meaningful work and helped them learn the cognitive tools necessary for success.

While educators today tell very different stories from this one, we believe that Feuerstein's (1980) story is somewhat similar to the stories of other great teachers today. Many seek to use powerful methods and strategies to lift students to embody a practical and optimistic spirit when they come to school, even though at times it is very difficult for them.

After working with Piaget as a young man and rising to the challenge to prepare people, many of whom had great difficulty, for successful lives, Feuerstein (1980) developed a method to teach all. His method has now been well researched and used around the world, primarily with at-risk youth. It is called mediated learning, and seems to provide some of the answers about creating high achieving courageous learners. Currently, some 50 years after the development of this approach, it is used with learners of all ages, birth through adult. This method, described below, is a part of the foundation of powerful tools that have been used successfully with courageous learners.

LEARNING OCCURS IN 2 WAYS:

1) Interaction directly with the environment, and

2) Coaching, or mediating, important learning principles and strategies.

All human beings must have coaching from a more experienced adult before they can begin to learn from direct interaction in the world.

ADAPTED FROM FEUERSTEIN, 1980

Mediated/Coached Learning

The mediated approach to teaching is at once a method that "makes sense" and yet represents a research based method for classroom use. This view might be considered to be positioned between the authoritarian and "laid back" methods and is more closely related to the teaching of a guide, or coach, a special kind of coach. The teacher as mediator/coach uses many opportunities in a day to guide students to independence through this method.

Donna's Story From A Mediated Classroom

Author Donna has been using the science of mediating learning in the classroom for over a decade. We have found that while all students benefit, courageous learners gain more than other students from this method. It offers Feuerstein's (1980) parameters for guiding student learning as a well researched framework from which teachers (such as the author) develop their own adaptation. In Donna's example from the classroom, a cognitive intervention with 20 strategies for thinking were taught to the second graders three times a week. The cognitive strategies were then used in academic subjects, social situations, and life examples during the rest of the week as appropriate and necessary. The students experienced gains in all of the areas listed below.

The items reflect areas that are important for school success and that are not often areas where at-risk students have success when they enter school as young children. Unfortunately, while performance on these items is a requirement for school success, often explicit guidance on items such as these, is absent from our schools. Therefore those students who came to school lacking them, often still lack these skills in high school and constitute a growing number of at-risk youth today. However, it is important to note that the areas covered here are skills that can be taught in any school, as they were in author Donna's intervention.

What follows throughout this chapter are specific tools that we have used with courageous learners to increase appropriate behavior and boost achievement gains. These 7 tools are a part of our *BrainSMART Thinking* (in press, b)book and video set what will be available in 2001. *BrainSMART Thinking* includes over 25 thinking tools and ideas for innovative implementation!

Principles of Mediated Teaching

There are 3 major principles in a classroom where the teacher is a mediational coach for learning and thinking. First, the environment is arranged

Teach Thinking Tools Explicitly

See Results!

Classroom Behavior Profile

Follows directions without need for additional explanation.

Spontaneously corrects own mistakes.

Has little fear of failure.

Makes minimal erasures and errors.

Demands precision and accuracy from self.

Tolerant of opinion of others.

Spontaneously uses helping devices—
(i.e. dictionary, other person).

Adequately attends to a given task.

Copes with problems adequately.

Automatically checks own work.

Takes responsibility for supplies.

Spontaneously uses taught vocabulary and/or concepts.

Gives details within the story when asked to identify the main idea.

Writes or draws with appropriate use of space on page.

Finishes work on time.

Organizes work area.

Applies what he/she learns in other areas.

Displays enthusiasm for learning.

Demonstrates interest in the responses of other students.

Adopted from Wilson, 1996

for maximum interaction among teacher and students, students learning together, and students interacting with engaging materials. The classroom is an exciting laboratory for learning. In this stimulating environment, learning takes place in two primary ways: 1) learning is constructed in the mind of the student independently, and 2) experienced mediators guide students to learn how to learn so that they can make good use of interdependent experiences.

The teacher as mediator/coach is a partner in relationship with courageous learners. The teacher is consistently engaging in their own challenging problems and is in touch with the joys and difficulties that arise when learning happens. Therefore, courageous teachers model practical optimism as they guide at-risk learners to problem solve. Additionally, teachers who use this method help students become better thinkers by questioning, rather than only lecturing. You probably recognize this as the technique Socrates and other great teachers have used throughout the ages. It engages students while it makes them aware of their process of thinking as they learn to question themselves.

Lastly, installing and creating habits for thinking and learning are at the very front and center of the classroom. This is critical for at-risk learners. If they do not have an opportunity to create important thinking and learning habits, they will continue to fall behind and experience greater and greater frustration.

7 Very Necessary Thinking Skills – Not Optional!

In both life and academics there are some skills of thinking that constitute the 20% that gets 80% of the results! The following necessary skills are those that author Donna has noticed are often not used by students who have difficulty at school. Some, or all of these skills were described by the referring teachers as being weak in approximately 90% of the referrals that Donna received when she was working as a school psychologist who diagnosed learning difficulties and evaluated students for possible special education placement.

When we taught 20 thinking tools to second grade students in the regular education classroom we quickly saw a need for explicitly teaching all students to understand the process of successful problem solving. The following excerpt from author Donna's (1996) article in the *"Journal of Cognitive Education"* tells the story of the first thinking lesson at the beginning of the school year.

Seven Selected Thinking Tools
For Academic and Lifelong Success

Optimism

Systematic Gathering of Information

Planning

Controlling Self-Expression

Self-Regulation

Understanding Space

Understanding Time

A Lesson for Us – The Teachers

"The second graders were shown two pictures of learners, and asked which one showed a focused, non-impulsive learner. Both pictures had balloons with the words "Listen Class" from the teacher. One picture portrayed a girl sitting still at a desk, focused, appearing still and, seemingly, ready to listen while the other showed a child wildly waving her arm in the air and kicking papers with her foot. Ten out of 20 of these students reasoned that, in fact, the latter learner was focused and ready to learn because she was shown trying to get her teacher's attention."

As we thought, about 50% of this class of second graders did not understand how to prepare to gather information in the situation. We expected that the same percentage of students were at-risk of difficulty their second grade year. The 50% of students who did not know how to approach this learning task, was the at-risk group. Because these students did not know how to "do school" when they came initially, and had had no class where they learned how, they were falling behind in most subjects. Many were also often getting into trouble as well. We found that many began to improve their process quickly when they were taught how to learn more effectively in all situations.

♥ Idea for Reflection

Do you have students who had coaching to develop these seven thinking tools? Which two are the most necessary for next steps?

1.

2.

Help Students Develop Practical Optimism

After a Failure – Develop Optimistic Thinking

This is <u>not personal</u>.

It is <u>not permanent</u>.

It is also <u>not pervasive</u>.

⚙ Tool 1: Practical Optimism

The first key to creating thinking classrooms is practical optimism. Have you ever had a day when you were in a negative state? How quickly did your students detect that in you, and how did they respond? Often, they are soon hitting your "hot buttons." How much learning happens? Very little. Think of a time when you were in a positive state. What happened to learning in your classroom? Practical optimism is a central factor in ensuring effective learning.

Goodlad's (1984) research in over 1,000 classrooms led him to describe the environments as "flat." The truth is that eliciting and sustaining healthy positive learning is the first step to creating classrooms for courageous learners. In today's classrooms this may be difficult.

The Harvard School of Public Health (Childre, Martin, & Beech, 1999) identifies depression as the fourth leading cause of disease burden in 1990 and predicts that by 2020 it will be the single leading cause. At the same time 75-90% of all doctor visits are for stress related disorders. Harvard researcher, Kessler (Elias, 1999) suggests that 23% of students experience depression and that pessimism, a precursor to depression is a learned theory of reality. Additionally, 60-80% of students with learning disabilities exhibit symptoms of depression.

Three key factors determine how we interpret life's events: 1) people with a pessimistic style of thinking think that failure is *personal*, then these people decide that there is something wrong with them that created the situation, 2) pessimistic people think that the results are *pervasive* and color every part of life, and 3) these pessimistic style thinkers believe that the results of a failure are *permanent* and may never be changed, or altered.

How they answer these questions is a key determinant of their level of optimism and academic achievement. For example, if the child interprets failure as being caused by their lack of ability, which is a permanent statement of fact that effects their whole life they may develop pessimism. Hence, the BrainSMART principle, "never question ability, always improve strategy." By teaching students that failure is a temporary setback that can be overcome by learning effective strategies, we help students to build the sense of mastery that drives optimism and self esteem. The key is to help students feel good by doing well and hitting the "save key" on their successes. (See Chapter 5 for this exercise.) In BrainSMART teaching we guide students in building a "success file" filled with concrete and authentic academic achievements.

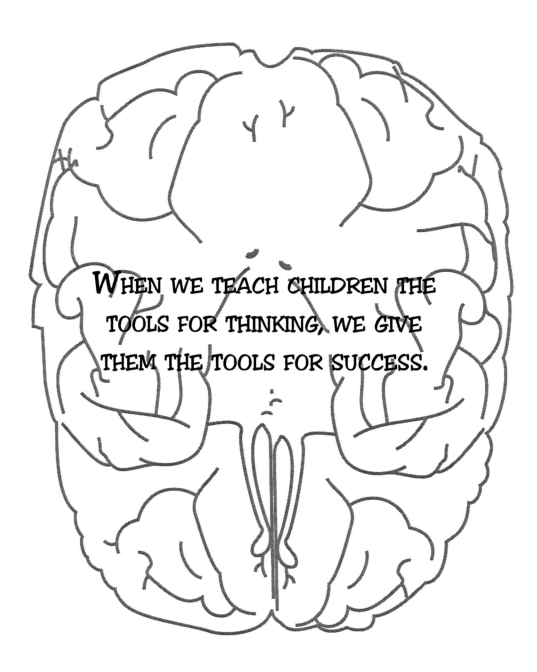

When we teach children the tools for thinking, we give them the tools for success.

Children learn pessimism from parents, teachers, and the media (Seligman, 1995). They become adults and recycle it to their children. Young people often develop what motivational researchers call "learned helplessness." After repeated failure, students who suffer from this problem decide they are not capable of performing well on academic tasks. Often, they are not motivated to even begin tasks at school, because they feel they won't succeed. These students may seem negative, pessimistic, or withdrawn. Eventually, they may drop out of school. Every two students who drop out cost their communities $1.5 million dollars. The cost of pessimism, and otherwise poor thinking, is great.

💡 Idea for Reflection

List 3 ways you can use this tool in your classroom.

1.

2.

3.

89

Systematic Search

Our Challenge – "I have impulsive students showing up in my class that don't even know how to begin to do a simple lesson!"

Definition - Appropriate exploratory behavior that is organized in a way that leads to a planned and well expressed response.

Teacher's Intent – To facilitate a need within the student to use an organized method to gather resources for solving any problem in life and school. As guide, the teacher amplifies the process of gathering data in an organized way.

♪ Tool 2: Systematic Search

Most of us would agree that being skilled at systematically solving problems is not something that we are innately able to do at birth. It is a learned skill. However, many at-risk students come to school without this skill and, as with many other necessary skills, it is not taught explicitly as a skill that most everyone can further develop. We teach this aspect of problem solving in three phases: a) *systematic search*, b) *planning*, and c) *controlling self - expression.* All need to be used systematically and habitually for maximum benefit. To teach at-risk (and some other students) how to systematically solve a problem, notice the sample lesson with steps for teaching students how to accomplish *systematic search.*

Steps For A Lesson

Step 1: As a class discuss what it means to *gather information* about a problem. How does good problem solving include this phase of the process? How is this different from impulsive action?

Step 2: As a class choose a topic as an example to study, i.e. healthy eating.

Step 3: Mindmap ways to *gather information* about the topic. (For more information about mindmapping and other visual techniques see *BrainSMART Strategies for Boosting Test Scores,* 2000.)

Examples from students might be to get a book on nutrition, go to a wellness doctor, take a class at the health department, ask a very healthy person, or explore it on the internet.

Step 4: Ask students the following question: "How can we use what we have learned about *gathering information* in Language Arts, or other classes, today? How can we gather information in our lives?

Step 5: After students have had a chance to *gather information,* ask them to work in pairs and share how they accomplished the task.

91

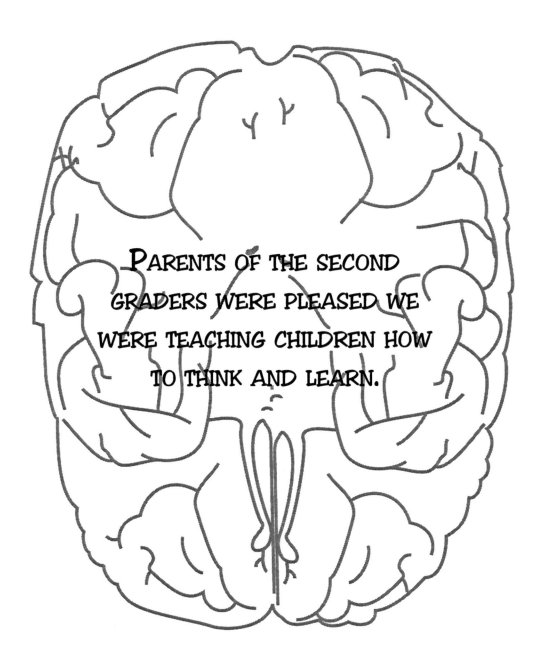

Parents of the second graders were pleased we were teaching children how to think and learn.

Sample Guiding Questions

What are the resources available to me to solve the problem?

What materials do I need to complete this exercise?

How do I plan to gather the necessary information for this paper?

When we have taught students in this process oriented approach, they have often said that it helps show them the way to be successful. With the emphasis on grades and tests, younger students often think that the only aspect of problem solving is *expression*, the last phase. Until thinking class, they often do not know that the care with which we gather information and make a plan often determine the outcome after expression!

When we have trained teachers using this approach, they think it is exciting and see that it makes a difference! Often these courageous teachers are surprised to see how focused educational systems seem to be on the product, rather than the process. We believe, along with many other teachers, that student products get better when they understand the process leading to the development of the product, or expression of knowledge.

ᕟ Idea for Reflection

List 3 ways you can use this tool in your classroom.

1.

2.

3.

Planning

Our Challenge – "Some students jump into the answer before they even think about planning their response. Others don't even begin!"

Definition - Appropriate planning behavior that is organized in a way that leads to a well expressed response.

Teacher's Intent – To facilitate a need within the student to use an organized method to plan for solving any problem in life and school. As guide, the teacher amplifies the <u>process </u>of planning in an organized way.

♪ Tool 3: Planning

After students have been introduced to systematic search and practiced using it as the first part of the process of problem solving, they are ready to practice planning as the second part of the process. As with all aspects of thinking, give students many chances to develop examples about when the planning phase of problem solving makes the difference between success and failure.

Steps for a Lesson

Step 1: Ask the students when in their lives has it been important for them to make a *plan* in order to succeed at something.

Step 2: Tell a story of two different families. One family makes a *plan* for the summer vacation and another does not.

Step 3: Have the students discuss possible scenarios that could happen with these two families.

Step 4: Ask the students what a good *plan* for a vacation includes.

Step 5: Mindmap the class *plan* as a group.

Step 6: Plan follow-up lessons that allow the students to be able to make a *plan* for success.

Sample Guiding Questions

What is my plan to solve this problem?

Have I mapped out my plan so I will have a visual of it?

Do I have what I need to implement the plan?

95

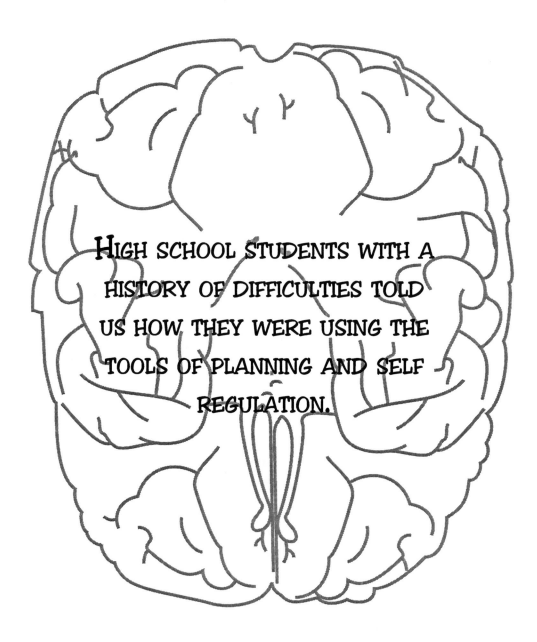

HIGH SCHOOL STUDENTS WITH A HISTORY OF DIFFICULTIES TOLD US HOW THEY WERE USING THE TOOLS OF PLANNING AND SELF REGULATION.

Learning to Make a Plan:
A Story Told Happily By Mother

After lessons such as these in gathering information and using it to make a good plan, many students we have taught tell stories of their use of these thinking blocks at home and school. Here is one parent's recollection of her daughter's journey to becoming a better problem solver while experiencing author Donna's coaching for learning in Sue's elementary school. Sue's parents were both very glad that the school offered classes in thinking where the knowledge and skills could be transferred to home, as well as school. Before she began to develop a systematic approach to problem solving and other thinking skills, she had great difficulty with schoolwork.

Sue:	*"Dad, you can do better if you use Systematic Planning. It will help you organize your desk better."*
Father:	*"I need to what? Hey, Mom, what in the world is Susie talking about?"*
Mother:	*"I didn't hear her. What did you say, Sue?"*
Sue:	*"I told Dad he should use Systematic Planning to help him get better organized."*
Father:	*"Where is she learning these skills and vocabulary?"*
Mother:	*"At school. Her teacher and others have begun using a learning to learn approach. They are planning to hold a meeting soon to see if parents want to join them by helping our children learn to learn at home."*
Sue:	*"In my class we're building a learning community and using building blocks and tools for thinking to make strategies so we don't have trouble learning."*
Mother:	*"So…what did you tell Dad?"*
Sue:	*"I just told him that if he uses Systematic Planning he will be able to decide on a strategy for organizing his stuff. Maybe he needs Self-Regulation, too!"*

Controlled Self-Expression

Our Challenge – "The answers some of our students give! It is as if they just give the first one off the top of their heads!"

Definition – A thoughtful response made after adequate exploration and planning is completed.

Teacher's Intent – To facilitate a need within the student to communicate in a way that will help them be successful at school and in life. As guide, the teacher amplifies the <u>process </u>of controlled expression.

♂ Tool 4: Controlled Self-Expression

When students understand and use systematic search and effective planning, they are ready to discuss and use controlled self-expression. As they add the third phase of problem solving to their practice, continue to question the students about the need for the first two phases so that they understand systematic search, planning, and self-expression as a connected process.

Steps for a Lesson

Step 1: State to the whole class, "Today as we take a test I would like for you to be aware of your outlook."

Step 2: Ask them to remember the discussions and exercises for creating an optimistic outlook.

Step 3: Remind them that as they work on the test to remember to breathe deeply when necessary and to recall that they are in their "Success Seats". For more on the Success Seat Tool see *BrainSMART Strategies for Boosting Test Scores* (2000).

Step 4: Discuss the importance of using *Controlled Self-Expression* even when it is difficult.

Sample Guiding Questions

Am I being impulsive in answering this question?

Have I considered others' point of view before making my response?

Have I rehearsed my response so that I won't get emotionally blocked when I speak?

Did I edit my paper before turning it in?

Self-Regulation

Our Challenge – "We are getting more students each year who come to school without the necessary self- control to be able to succeed."

Definition – The skill to control and pace one's responses in a way so as to be successful in school and life.

Teacher's Intent – To facilitate a need within the student to self-regulate. As guide, the teacher amplifies the <u>process</u> of self-regulation.

🎵 Tool 5: Self-Regulation

Would you agree that understanding how each of us is responsible for controlling and monitoring our own learning is a very important frame for our students to develop? Using the language of thinking and learning is very important for courageous learners. After a BrainSMART workshop for students, the authors recently heard a young student exclaim, "Now I that I have self-regulation I really have control of my own brain!" His delight captures the essence of excitement that people of ages have as they discover this truth as they use the language of learning and thinking.

Steps for a Lesson

Step 1: In this lesson today I want you to pay attention to the way you get the job completed.

Step 2: Ask the question "has anyone heard of the term *self-regulation*?"

Step 3: "Yes, *self-regulation* is about taking control of your life and learning experiences."

Step 4: "On our lesson today, I want you to notice your level of optimism we begin the lesson."

Step 5: Ask "Do we need to do some exercises to help us get into a more optimistic state to begin the lesson?" A part of *self-regulation* is being optimistic about the task. We have control of our perception!

Step 6: I also want you to notice the time. How do you use the time you have to complete the lesson? Do you begin on time? Do you finish?

Step 7: I look forward to hearing from you after the lesson. I want us to reflect on your use of *self-regulation* to be optimistic and complete the task.

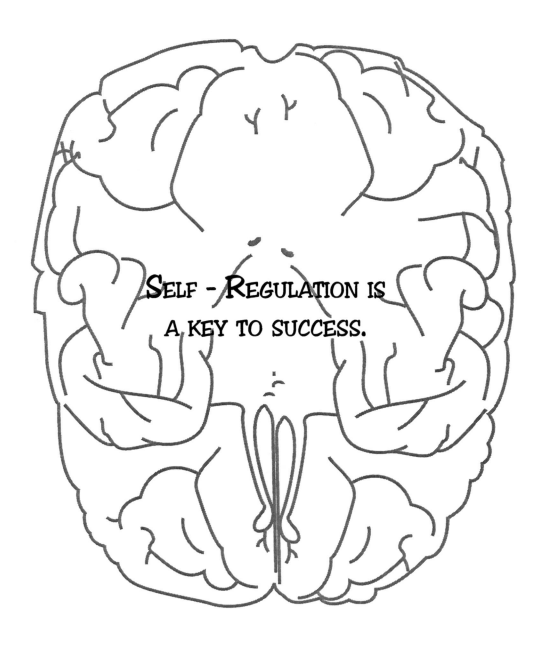

SELF - REGULATION IS
A KEY TO SUCCESS.

Sample Guiding Questions

Am I taking as much time as I need to in order to be accurate and precise when necessary?

Have I observed the cues so I know what appropriate behavior is in this situation?

Do I have a stoplight in my mind that shows red when I need to stop; yellow when I need to be careful; and green when I can start?

The Story of Mark: A Courageous Sophomore

As we mentioned earlier, while Sue, in the scenario previously mentioned, learned important thinking skills in elementary school because her school made it a priority, some students do not acquire these important skills at home or in school. Mark's story is about a 10th grade boy, whose special education teacher coached him and his classmates to be better thinkers and learners for school and life. Mark and his classmates were in a class labeled for students with the label learning disabled and seriously emotionally disturbed. Coaching the students to be better thinkers, Mark's teacher guided the students to better organize, plan, and regulate themselves at school and in their lives. Mark's teacher proudly tells his story.

> *"Mark told us that he had used what he learned in her class to control himself when another student tried to start a fight. He remarked that when approached he took a moment to reflect, gather information, and decided it wasn't worth hitting and getting expelled for because he would have to repeat the 10th grade. He went on to explain that he used organization at home to structure his finances and help his family to do the same for the month. Additionally, he reported that the thinking class had helped him to plan and write an "A" essay in literature class and to discover what information was relevant from the internet. Most importantly, Mark told his teacher that not only had he accomplished the tasks, but that he had learned how to control his behavior; help organize his life, and produce his schoolwork as a result of thinking class. Mark's teacher then amplified the importance of this incident by exclaiming to Mark that he had accomplished something very important in*

MARK'S EXAMPLE ILLUSTRATES THE POWER OF GREAT TEACHING. HIS TEACHER, MRS. WADE, EXPLICITLY TAUGHT THE MOST IMPORTANT THINKING PRINCIPLES IN ORDER FOR HIM AND HIS CLASSMATES TO TRANSFORM THEIR LIVES FOR SUCCESS.

his life. That is, he had been thoughtful, not impulsive, and has learned how to organize his thoughts. And, very importantly, once you have done these things, you can do them every time!"

This story reveals the power of thinking tools when they are used with high school courageous learners on a daily basis, and when the students are encouraged to use the skills outside of class, as well as in class. It brings to mind the *power* of learning how to reflect on one's own behavior and thinking!

♀ Idea for Reflection

List 3 ways you can use this tool in your classroom.

1.

2.

3.

Understanding Space Concepts

Our Challenge – "A lot of our students get in trouble because they get in other people's personal space in a disrespectful way."

Definition – Understanding how space is a very important part of life and school.

Teacher's Intent – To facilitate the students' need and skill to be able to get around in the world in a way that they will be able to be successful. As guide, the teacher amplifies the <u>process</u> of understanding spatial concepts.

♪ Tool 6: Understanding Space

In his new book, *A Biological Brain In a Cultural Classroom,* Sylwester (2000) notes that space and time are important issues in classroom management. Ask any teacher of courageous learners how important it is for learners to be able to navigate through space without bumping into others and how to use space when constructing a work of art. This is core understanding that students need to get a grasp of point of view as well as self and other.

Steps for a Lesson (told from the teacher's point of view)

Step 1: As I gently bump into the door facing me, I ask the students, "Am I using *Space Concepts* well at the moment?"

Step 2: The students will often laugh as I frame the lesson in my mistake. I might question, "Do any of you ever have difficulty like me because of a problem with use of *Space Concepts*?"

Step 3: Ask the class "What are some problems that can occur as a result?"

Step 4: After they have had a chance to reflect and answer the question, I often ask, "How do we use *Space Concepts* when we do paper, or computer work?"

Step 5: Here it is great to encourage careful examination of spacing procedures and readability of papers.

Step 6: Encourage students to consider their use of space in the classroom and in their lives elsewhere.

Billy's Story

"I didn't know that space concepts were so important until we studied them in thinking class. Now, I use space in the cafeteria line and don't get in trouble for bumping people in the line. My papers are neater now. I make rows when I write and my teacher says she can read it better. My mother uses space concepts when she drives. She always keeps space after other cars in front of us. It is fun to be studying something so important for people all ages."

107

Understanding of Space Concepts

Lack of Skill

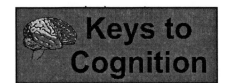

Understanding of Space Concepts

Skilled

www.brainsmart.com

Sample Guiding Questions

Am I being offensive to others by standing too close when I'm in conversation them?

Do my papers indicate that my writing is too "squeezed together" or "spaced out" to be read clearly?

What does spatial orientation have to do with point of view? How is this important in literature? How is this important in war history?

Idea for Reflection

List 3 ways you can use this tool in your classroom.

1.

2.

3.

Understanding Time Concepts

Our Challenge – "Many of our students have no concept of time. They are often late to class and late turning in their papers."

Definition – Understanding how time is a very important part of life and school.

Teacher's Intent – To facilitate the students' need and skill at understanding time so that they will be able to be successful. As guide, the teacher amplifies the <u>process </u>of understanding time concepts.

♂ Tool 7: Understanding Time

Both understanding of time and space, more than many concepts, must be mediated, or coached, and do have a strong cultural component. For example, reflect on this question. What child could learn how to use time to their benefit in relationships and to reach goals, without some guidance about how this is done within the culture. It is important to help courageous learners begin to feel a sense of time as a part of understanding it. Also, it is necessary to help them use experiences to understand that time is subject to emotions. For example, it seems to fly, or drags on, depending on one's emotional state. Given this, is it smart for courageous learners to wear a timepiece and notice it?

Steps for a Lesson

Step 1: Look at your watch and make a big deal of the time. Ask the students "What does 1 minute feel like?"

Step 2: Give students a chance to give answers.

Step 3: Ask them to experiment with you and experience the way time feels different when we are and are not busy.

Step 4: Tell the students that you are going to give them 1 minute of time with their eyes closed for quiet time. Ask them to please raise their hand when they think 1 minute has lapsed.

Step 5: After you make a big deal of the difference (it has always happened for groups of students), you set it up again.

Step 6: This time give them a task to help develop habitual behavior, i.e. a drill, over something they have learned. Ask them to respond as rapidly as possible.

Step 7: Again, make a big deal of the start time and ask them to time themselves again with their internal clock while working and raise a hand when they think 1 minute is over.

Step 8: Afterward, discuss the emotional aspect of keeping track of time and the need for timepieces.

Step 9: As a whole group ask students to give examples of problems they have experienced when they forgot to pay attention to this important aspect of life.

111

Understanding Time Concepts

Lack of Skill

Understanding Time Concepts

Skilled

www.brainsmart.com

Sample Guiding Questions

Do I often get in trouble for being late?

How am I doing at paying attention to time when it is necessary?

Do I use a timepiece to check time when I have a deadline to meet?

Am I pacing myself well on tests?

Idea for Reflection

List 3 ways you can use this tool in your classroom.

1.

2.

3.

Summary:

There are over 25 thinking tools in the BrainSMART Thinking Program. We hope that this introduction to 7 thinking tools will be as enriching for you as it is for us as we use them in our lives and teaching. If your students need more BrainSMART thinking tools, we recommend our new book *BrainSMART Thinking Tools* which will be published in 2001. This new book will be featured in our 5 day Institute. This Institute is called BrainSMART Thinking: Higher Test Scores - Safer Schools. For more information visit us at www.brainsmart.com

Chapter 5
BrainSMART
Tools
for
Learning

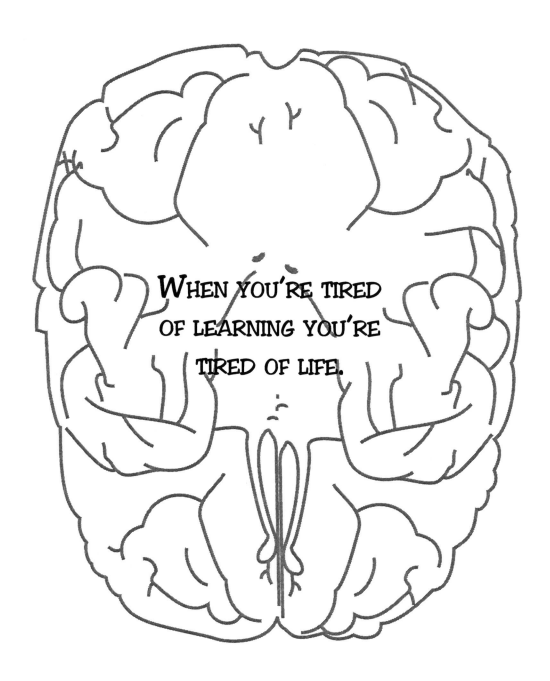

WHEN YOU'RE TIRED
OF LEARNING YOU'RE
TIRED OF LIFE.

Meet Mary and Linda

Two students in Wilmington, Delaware embody the spirit, belief, and methods congruent with this chapter on learning. Author Donna had the privilege of working with our students (we will call them Mary and Linda) as a co-teacher and learning coach. As a part of the experience, Donna guided Mary, Linda, and other students in their special education classroom as they learned tools to help them learn at school and home.

Several days after Donna had taught Mary, and her classmates our multi modal memory tool called Memory Pegs (given later in this chapter), Mary and Linda ran to Donna in the school cafeteria and began to "show-off," illustrating what they remembered from the exercise. Mary and Linda remembered the entire Memory Pegs exercise. They were so proud! More importantly, they used the power of thinking about their thinking, to remind us that they can learn new things at school!

This is a very important moment in the lives of Mary and Linda! It is especially important because their classroom is designed for students who score within the measured I.Q. range between 50 and 70, with 100 being average. The adaptive behavior of these students is also measured at below the normal range. We believe, along with a growing number of educators and parents, that functional intelligence improves greatly when students actually believe that they are good at learning! So, Mary, Linda, and their classmates have reason to believe that they are getting smarter, and we agree.

In this chapter on learning, you will learn 10 key practices from neuroscience and cognitive education. When we visit classrooms across the U.S. that are applying these keys in their schools and classrooms, we see that they are lifting the lives of their at-risk students, as well as others. Then we share nineteen top tools for boosting student learning and achievement through better memory. The tools and ideas in this chapter are currently being used in the successful three year state initiative to decrease the number of students at-risk of dropping out of school in Florida as well as in many other classrooms across the land.

Ten Keys to Learning and Teaching

As indicated in Chapter 4, the research on students at-risk indicates that these students must become better learners and thinkers. Those who have opportunity to engage in explicit instruction toward those ends do have a better chance of success in school and life. Those who never have the chance to learn to learn and become better thinkers tend to get further and further behind at school. In classrooms where the following 10 keys are applied, we

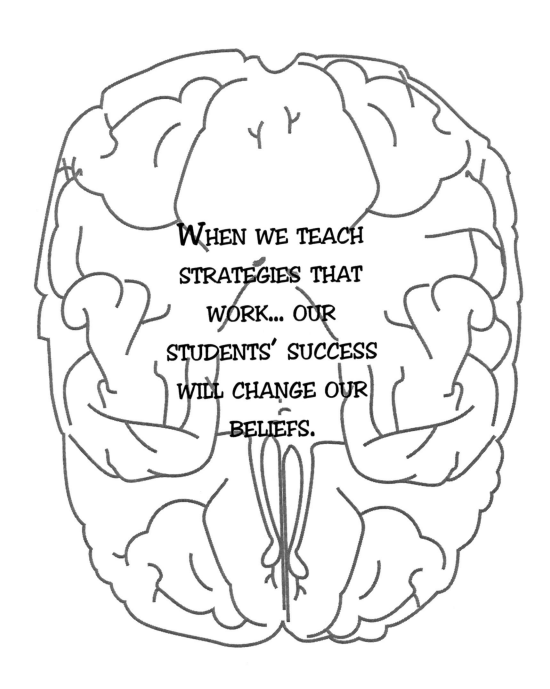

WHEN WE TEACH STRATEGIES THAT WORK... OUR STUDENTS' SUCCESS WILL CHANGE OUR BELIEFS.

Ten Keys to
BRAINSMART *Teaching*

Belief	Believe in your students' potential to succeed.
Read	Read the distinct learning styles of each student.
Align	Build rapport and teach in the styles in which each student learns best.
Inspire	Model the behaviors and love of learning that inspires achievement.
No put-downs	Avoid sarcasm, remove threat.
State	Trigger and sustain peak learning states.
Meaning	Make learning meaningful and relevant to the learners' real world.
Attention	Sustain attention through enthusiasm, variety and feedback.
Retention	Use multiple retention strategies to make learning stick.
Transfer	Teach with transfer in mind to secure recall during the test and in life.

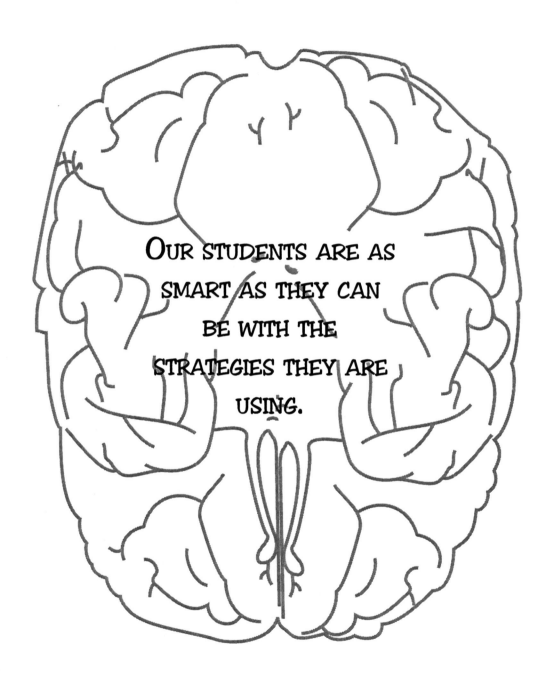

OUR STUDENTS ARE AS
SMART AS THEY CAN
BE WITH THE
STRATEGIES THEY ARE
USING.

experience students learning to learn and applying the tools to academic content.

1: Belief is ever so important! In our workshops the authors hear great teachers share how courageous learners are succeeding in their classes. Their powerful stories reveal that the teachers are committed to helping these students learn how to learn and think. The result is that the students are learning and enjoying the process. Guskey's (1994) research on professional development and student achievement indicates that teachers change our beliefs about practices that affect student achievement as we learn and practice new methods.

2: Read the learning styles of your students! One of the parts of BrainSMART workshops that participants enjoy the most is learning how to read the verbal and nonverbal cues of students that indicate their learning and thinking style. For example, author Marcus is a highly visual learner and when he was a schoolboy in England he would look up at the ceiling when the teacher asked him a question. The teacher would exclaim, "The answer is not written on the ceiling!" Of course, a BrainSMART teacher would know that visual learners tend to look up to access their visual memory system. A quick version of the R.E.A.D. model for observing is R. for rate of speech, E. for eye movements, A. for actions and gestures, and D. for dialogue. For more on this method see *BrainSMART Strategies for Boosting Test Scores* (2000).

3: Align Build rapport and teach in the styles in which each student learns best. Sylwester (1995), in his book that addresses the neurobiology of classroom management, notes the importance of understanding and teaching different styles of learners in our classrooms. For many years savvy educators have noticed that a very large percentage of at-risk students are kinesthetic and visual, and this number is growing. In her book, *Smart Moves*, researcher Hannaford (1995) notes that only 15% of teachers teach in these modalities as a rule.

4: Inspire a love of learning and student achievement! Recently, author Donna listened as an elementary student at

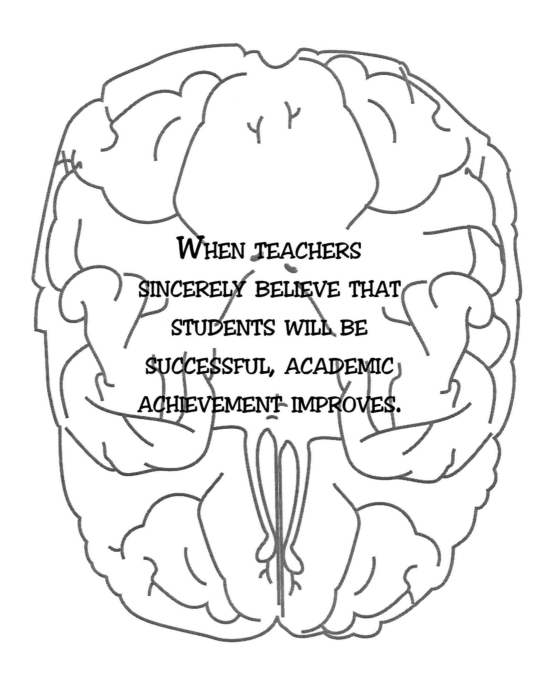

WHEN TEACHERS
SINCERELY BELIEVE THAT
STUDENTS WILL BE
SUCCESSFUL, ACADEMIC
ACHIEVEMENT IMPROVES.

Switlik Elementary School in Marathon, Florida told about his success at school. We'll call our second grader Mark. Mark ran to "Dr. Donna" and "The Brain Guy" who were visiting Mark, his classmates, and teachers at Switlik. As he spoke to her, his tone reflected high energy and excitement as he told Donna how he had used the *eyes up* strategy noted later in this chapter to remember how to spell a word on the spelling test earlier that day. He gasped, "Wow! I've never made an A on a spelling test until today! Strategies help!" Bravo to his teachers who are teaching Mark and his classmates strategies for success.

5: No put-downs

Avoid sarcasm and remove threat. We know that when we feel threatened, the brain shuts down and learning decreases. Research suggests that for many people sharp sarcasm, or petty put-downs has the same impact on the heart as a heavy workout, or a mild myocardial infarction.

6: State

Trigger and sustain peak learning states. Three major keys to positive states are physiology, food, and focus. In BrainSMART workshops we model the use of these 3 keys for increasing positive states in the classroom. For many at-risk students, movement is critical for learning and to keep the body in balance. In the BrainSMART nutrition segment, keys to good nutrition, such as balance in protein, fruits, vegetables, and healthy essential fatty acids, are discussed. To sustain peak states in the classroom always consider "What's important now?" and "What's useful and positive?"

7: Meaning

Make learning meaningful and relevant to the learners' real world. The human brain runs two important systems in the learning process. The first, is to focus attention on what is most personally meaningful. Secondly, having focused, it saves what is most useful and relevant and deletes everything else. Haberman, in his classic work, *Star Teachers of Children In Poverty*, found that highly effective teachers focus on making the learning meaningful and engaging for their students.

123

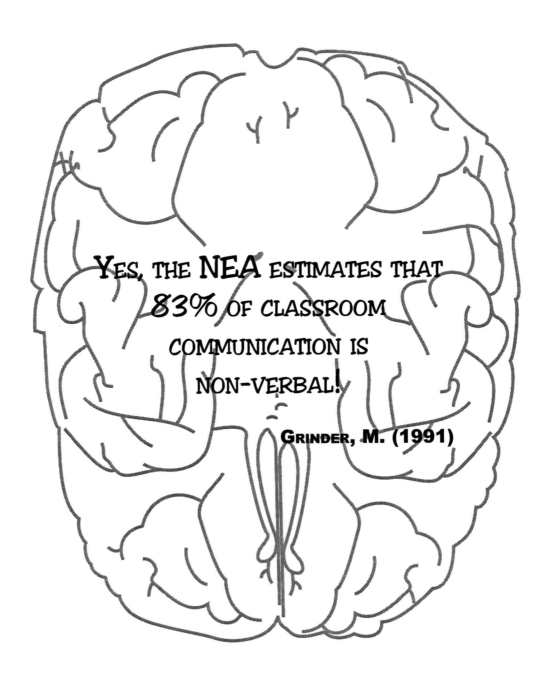

Research on how some students from poverty learn mathematics illuminates a powerful truth. Students learn best when the context is meaningful. For example, students were found to be able to perform well in mathematical calculations involving change owed after buying items at a candy store. When asked to do a similar exercise in an abstract form in a school setting they performed badly even though the calculation was identical.

Research also suggests that teaching isolated mathematics skills through lecture and ditto sheets is prone to failure for producing meaningful learning that results in high student achievement. For example, in Japan, where some of the highest mathematics scores were recorded in the TIMSS Study, 40% of instruction time was spent practicing routine procedures, 15% applying procedures in new situations, and 45% of instruction time was spent creating new procedures and analyzing new situations. Therefore, students were creating meaning themselves while being guided by their teachers (as cited in Stigler and Hiebert, 1999).

In contrast, in the U.S. students spend 90% of their time practicing routine procedures. The remainder of the time (10%) is spent applying the procedures in various problems. Virtually no time is spent inventing new procedures. The study reported that the U.S. eighth graders ranked 28th out of 41 nations in mathematics. Once again, we see that the *system* of teaching mathematics is producing these results for each nation.

8: Attention It is biologically impossible for the brain to learn if it is not paying attention. Some keys to generating attention are: Generate curiosity by using novelty, make information relevant, ask questions to engage your students, use variety, and use emotions.

9: Retention Use multiple retention strategies to make learning stick. The brain seemingly has a *save* key, to save data. We learn how to hit this button by using specific strategies. Enjoy using these nineteen BrainSMART memory strategies ready for you and your students to use and remember!

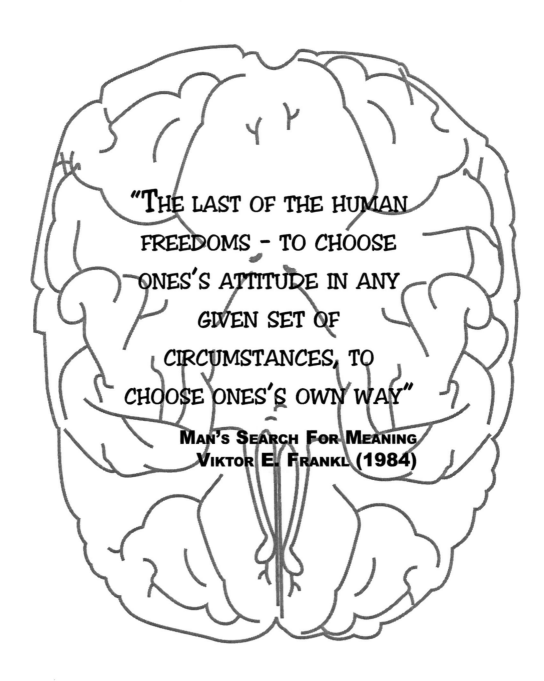

"THE LAST OF THE HUMAN
FREEDOMS - TO CHOOSE
ONES'S ATTITUDE IN ANY
GIVEN SET OF
CIRCUMSTANCES, TO
CHOOSE ONES'S OWN WAY"

MAN'S SEARCH FOR MEANING
VIKTOR E. FRANKL (1984)

✐ **10: Transfer**   Teach with transfer in mind to secure recall during the test and in life. The bottom line of learning is transferring it from the classroom to the test, and, often more importantly, from the classroom to life. A key to making transfer happen is to help our students develop the skill of "thinking about our thinking." In education, we call this skill metacognition. Studies have shown this skill to be the "Number 1" characteristic of students who are high achievers. And, it is both teachable and learnable by over 99% of our students.

Remember STAR TEACHERS GO FOR IT:

S   **Seven**
T   **Twenty Minutes**
A   **Association**
R   **Rehearsal**

T   **Ten Pegs**
E   **Eyes Up**
A   **Alliteration**
C   **Color**
H   **Highlighting**
E   **Emotion**
R   **Rap**
S   **Stories**

G   **Graphics**
O   **Organizers**

F   **First Letter Cueing**
O   **Open House Technique**
R   **Rocket List**

I   **Index Cards**
T   **Tunes**

Nineteen Memory Tools You Can Easily Use

These nineteen tools are classroom-tested ones that you can use immediately to help your students hit the *save* key. The acronym we use is "STAR TEACHERS GO FOR IT". Let's look now, at the nineteen tools represented by this acronym:

S ⇨ Seven

Research by Harvard's George Miller (1956) indicates that the human brain can store about seven bits of information in short-term memory. Notice all the references to seven in literature: the seven seas, the seven hills of Rome, even the very successful book *The Seven Habits of Highly Effective People* (Covey, 1989). Once, when we returned to England, we discovered that the phone company had changed telephone numbers from seven to eight digits. The result was that many people were unable to remember telephone numbers. This number is less than seven for younger students. A seven-year-old can retain about five chunks, and a five-year old only two chunks.

> *Action:* In your classroom, break all your information down into a maximum of seven bits (less for younger students). This will greatly increase the likelihood of your information being retained.

T ⇨ Twenty Minutes

Researcher Tony Buzan (1983) highlights the fact that the optimum learning time for many people is twenty minutes. When classes or lectures go beyond this, the brain begins a steady decline in terms of attention and retention potential. Notice that many television shows are about twenty minutes long, punctuated with commercials. Research also indicates that there is much more retention of the first things you say, (called *primacy*), and the last things you say (called *recency*).

> *Action:* Teach your classes in twenty-minute chunks of time, presenting the most important information first and last.

Home Pegs

You can use familiar surroundings of your own home to remember even more pegs! Here are examples of objects you can use.

Kitchen	Living Room
Refrigerator	Bookshelf
Microwave	Couch
Sink	Lamp
Dishwasher	TV
Oven	Table
Bathroom	Bedroom
Bathtub	Laundry Basket
Toilet	Curtain
Mirror	Picture
Sink	Bed
Towel Rack	Wardrobe

Front Door
Rocket - to connect home list
to rocket list

Exercise:

1. **Practice moving quickly forwards and backwards through your own personal home peg list.**

2. **Practice connecting your body list to your home list and your rocket list.**

A ⇨ Association

The brain works best when it can associate new information with existing information. This is critical for both meaning and retention. For example, when author Marcus teaches young children about being in positive states, he get them to visualize Bugs Bunny, and ask them what associations they have with him as a character. They say he's fun, he's intelligent, he's flexible. So, we begin to associate a peak learning state with Bugs Bunny. This causes long-term retention and recall.

> *Action:* Always associate new information with information you know your students already have. Also, use the other tools listed below to help you be effective in this area.

R ⇨ Rehearsal

The brain works in waves of attention and downtime. In order for information to be retained, the brain needs to have focused attention for a period of time while it takes in data, and then downtime to cement it in memory. Rehearsal is an optimum method for ensuring that this happens. A simple way is for students to teach each other what they've just learned in the last ten or twenty minutes. Another way is for them to practice doing a presentation on the subject, as though they will give a talk on it later on. Essentially, information is a "use it or lose it" thing. The more you use the information, the more you hit the *save* key.

> *Action:* Having taught for periods of twenty minutes, ensure that you have plenty of downtime for rehearsal. Good techniques for this are mind-mapping, think & pair-share, and other techniques we will describe.

T ⇨ Ten Pegs

This technique was developed by the Greeks, and refined by the Romans. It has been used for centuries to ensure effective retention of information. It draws on the power of association we discussed earlier. To use *Ten pegs*, we simply associate a number with different parts of the body. With this particular system, we go from head to toe; number 1 being head, 2 shoulders, 3 heart, 4 belly, 5 hips, 6 backside, 7 thighs, 8 knees, 9 shins, and 10 toes. You can install this body peg list very easily with your students.

131

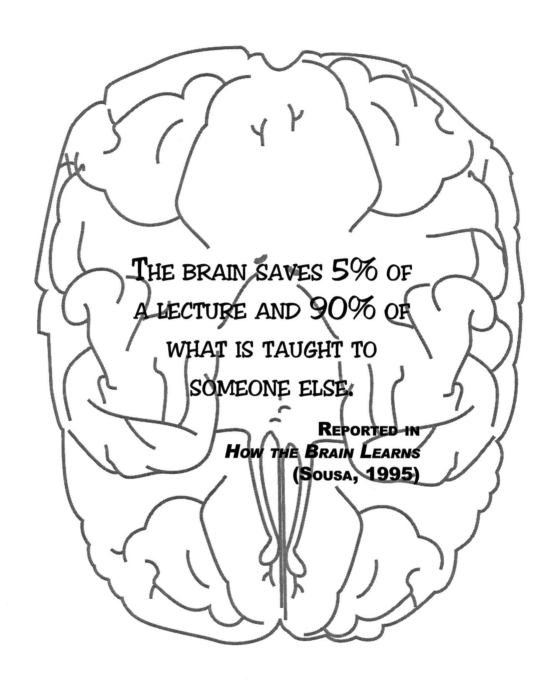

THE BRAIN SAVES 5% OF
A LECTURE AND 90% OF
WHAT IS TAUGHT TO
SOMEONE ELSE.

REPORTED IN
HOW THE BRAIN LEARNS
(SOUSA, 1995)

These pegs may be used to retain a whole variety of information, and can be effectively cleaned out after each usage.

> *Action:* Teach your students the ten pegs, and use them to retain some simple pieces of information. For example, retain tomato, molasses, steak, orange, banana, ice cream, mustard, string, band-aid, and eggs. Importantly, when your students succeed at this, do an "I Feel Good!" "YES!!" to cement that experience.

E ⇨ **Eyes Up**

Research indicates that most of the information we learn is learned visually. Have you ever sat down to take a test and found that your mind went blank? It's almost certain that many of your students have. One reason is that we've been told to look down at our own paper. When we look down, we switch off our brain's ability to access visual information.

> *Action:* Encourage your students to look up when they want to access information, and *please* delete from your repertoire, the phrase "The answer is not on the ceiling". As far as the student's brain is concerned, it *is* written there!

A ⇨ **Alliteration**

The brain's cortex is constantly scanning for patterns, and alliteration is a powerful way to make things more memorable. For example, we might describe teaching as being the art of modeling a *love* of *learning* and making information *meaningful* and *memorable*.

> *Action:* Use alliteration in your classes to increase attention and retention. Encourage your students to use their own alliteration patterns.

C ⇨ **Color**

The brain thinks in color, is stimulated by color, and has memory reinforced by the use of color. One simple example is 3M, who developed Post-it® Notes in yellow. They may have read some research that indicates that yellow is the first color that the brain notices. By using a wide variety of colors, you stimulate more of

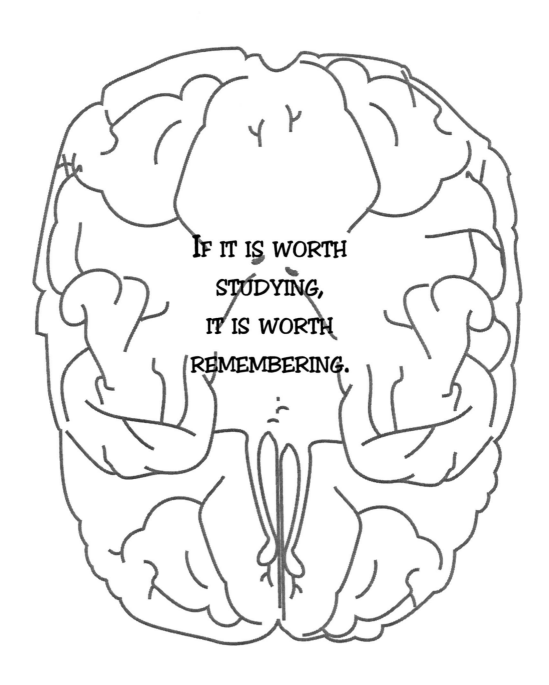

IF IT IS WORTH
STUDYING,
IT IS WORTH
REMEMBERING.

your students' brains. Researcher Tony Buzan (1983) draws attention to the fact that monochrome is one color, which, to the brain is similar to monotone, which is one tone. You have probably experienced the mind-numbing effect of monotone. Think of monochrome the same way.

> *Action:* Wherever possible, use a variety of colors to create a stimulating, memorable learning environment. Particularly during mind-mapping, use a minimum of five colors. Also, notice how television commercials, and other ads, make use of color. Remember that advertisers spend 138 billion dollars each year, and want to invest in those areas that produce the best results.

H ⇨ Highlighting

One of the ways to get the human brain to pay attention and retain information is to *highlight* that this is a very important fact. This is vital because, with the amount of data we expect our students to absorb, unless we highlight what is important, it is likely that they will remember some other information instead. A powerful way to do this is to get students, at any time during the class, to highlight the key points in what they have covered so far. To reduce stress, it is best to appoint a special highlighter for different parts of the presentation.

> *Action:* During your lesson planning, highlight the three critical factors you want your students to retain. Emphasize these in class. Appoint student highlighters to summarize highlights at key points.

E ⇨ Emotion

One of the keys for helping the brain to distinguish between what is important, and what is unimportant, is emotion. To test this for yourself, close your eyes and notice what you remember about the last five years. How much of it is dull, uninteresting, and boring? Your brain has probably hit the *delete* key for most of that, leaving you with saved memories that are highly emotional (whether positive, negative, or different), such as vacations. Use strong emotions to connect to information you want people to remember. Humor is particularly powerful in this regard. Notice how well kids can remember episodes from their favorite T.V. shows.

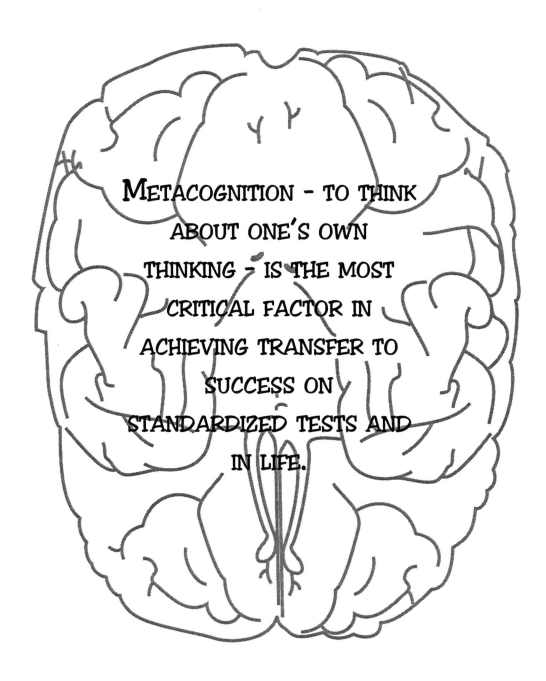

METACOGNITION – TO THINK ABOUT ONE'S OWN THINKING – IS THE MOST CRITICAL FACTOR IN ACHIEVING TRANSFER TO SUCCESS ON STANDARDIZED TESTS AND IN LIFE.

Action: Use positive emotions as you teach. Your enthusiasm can have an electrifyingly positive effect on retention. Use other emotions such as curiosity. For example, you might say something like "When we get back from lunch, you'll be fascinated by what we're going to learn."

R ⇨ Rap

One of the most powerful systems for helping the brain retain information is through rhyme and rhythm. Contemporary rap music is a strong way to do this. You may also notice that many of your students have an ability to remember vast amounts of lyrics from rap songs, or other music, and you can tap into the power of this.

Action: Get your students to create a rap song about information that is critical in the subject area that you are teaching.

S ⇨ Stories

As we say in our workshop, *stories stick*, while *facts fade*. The reason that stories may be so effective in creating retention is that they act in the way that the brain naturally learns best. They are visual, in that they tap into the seeing part of memory, they are associated, the students draw on their own mental pictures, and they are vivid experiences. The more vivid you make the experience, the stronger the encoding.

Action: Find stories that best illustrate the information that you want to have retained. Get the students to create stories.

G ⇨ Graphics

It is well known that a picture is worth a thousand words. At around a hundred and fifty words per minute, that's almost seven minutes of speech! So why not save your voice by using graphics? As we detailed earlier in the book, visual information can be stored very quickly and immediately in long-term memory. Cartoons are particularly memorable, because they are different. Graphics also allow the brain to *understand* information much more rapidly.

Action: Use graphics and pictures wherever possible in

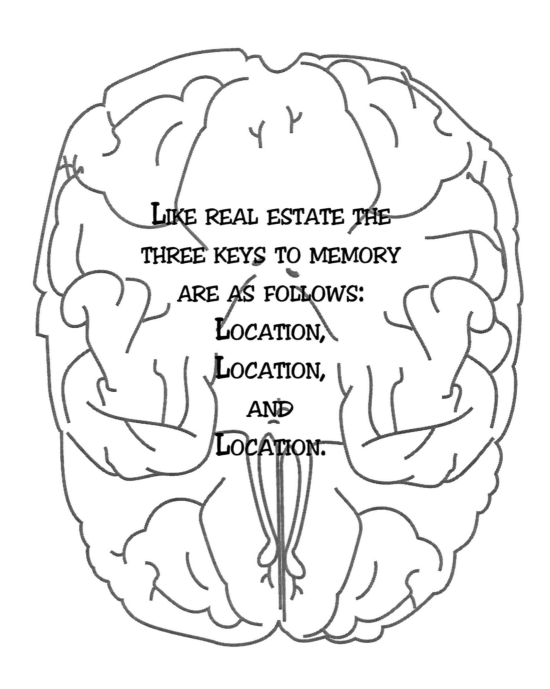

LIKE REAL ESTATE THE
THREE KEYS TO MEMORY
ARE AS FOLLOWS:
LOCATION,
LOCATION,
AND
LOCATION.

the course of your teaching. One of the most powerful systems is to use mind-mapping, which we will discuss next.

O ⇨ Organizers

Research indicates increases in retention when students use organizers to arrange information in a memorable way. One of the most effective forms of this is mind-mapping, developed by Tony Buzan (1983). This technique requires the use of the following key components:

- Make a strong central image.

- Have key facts branching out from that central image, as we see in the illustration.

- Use at least five colors.

- Print neatly, with only key words.

By using mind-mapping, huge increases in retention have been experienced in both school and business. Many students who do not work well auditorily can thrive by using mind maps. Boeing saved an estimated 11 million dollars by using mind-mapping to train engineers.

Action: Begin mind-mapping some of your lesson plans right away. One idea for engaging your students is to do what we call music mapping, where you get students to do a mind map of one of their favorite rock bands, or one of their favorite songs. This engages their interest.

F ⇨ First-Letter Cueing

Memory is a creative process, which can be triggered by getting one piece of the puzzle. First-letter cueing can be a highly effective way to do this. For example, in the BrainSMART process, we use the acronym SMART, for State, Meaning, Attention, Retention, Transfer. To remember these nineteen tools, we have STAR TEACHERS GO FOR IT.

Action: Use first-letter cueing to help students recall information. One classic is Every Good Boy Deserves Food.

Visual Pegs
Your Rocket List

Number	Peg	
1	Rocket	1 looks like a rocket ready for launch
2	Duck	2 looks like a duck
3	Triangle	A triangle has three sides
4	Horse	A horse has four legs
5	Hand	A hand has 5 fingers
6	Phone	6 looks like a phone
7	Boomerang	7 looks like a boomerang
8	Hourglass	8 looks like an hourglass
9	Cloud	Cloud 9
10	Knife and plate	Knife on your left – plate on right
11	Chopsticks	11 looks like chopsticks
12	Roses	A dozen roses
13	Witch	Bad luck
14	Valentines	February 14 is Valentine's Day
15	Tax Return	Yours in due on the 15th
16	Sugar	Sweet sixteen
17	Magazine	Seventeen is a magazine
18	Voting Booth	When you're 18, you can vote
19	Teenager	A 19-year old waves bye to teens
20	Spectacles	Spectacles can give you 20/20 vision

Exercise:
In your mind's eye run forwards and backwards through your rocket list.

O ⇨ Open House Technique

Here, you use an age-old system based on location memory. Imagine you had invited a guest to an open house, and you were leading them around your house. In each different part of the house, designate a memory-retention area. For example, in the kitchen, "one" might be the refrigerator, "two" might be the microwave, "three" might be the sink, "four" might be the dishwasher, and "five" might be the stove. In your mind's eye, as you create this, you can now add new information. For example, on the refrigerator, you might put "orange", on the microwave you might put "banana", on the sink, "pineapple", on the dishwasher you might put "pepper", and on the stove, "ten-dollar bill". You can use the open house technique to remember large numbers of items.

> *Action:* Help students create their own open house list, and then use it to remember key pieces of information.

R ⇨ Rocket List

Here, we once again tap into the visual imagination with twenty visual pegs. This is a great system for remembering large chunks of information.

> *Action:* Facilitate the students' learning of the rocket list, refer to often until it becomes second nature, and get students to break down the new information given during class, into a rocket list.

I ⇨ Index Cards

Index cards or flash cards can be an excellent way to focus on real learning. Our colleague, Howard Berg (Berg & Conyers, 1997), recommends this extensively in his trainings. On the front side of the card, write the question, such as "Who won the battle of Waterloo?" On the reverse side, write the answer, in this case, "The English". Keep a set of these flash or index cards, which you can carry with you anywhere. The beauty of this system is that, as soon as you have learned something, you remove it from the deck. This way, you avoid spending time reviewing information you already know.

> *Action:* Encourage your students to develop index or flash cards for the key pieces of information that you want them

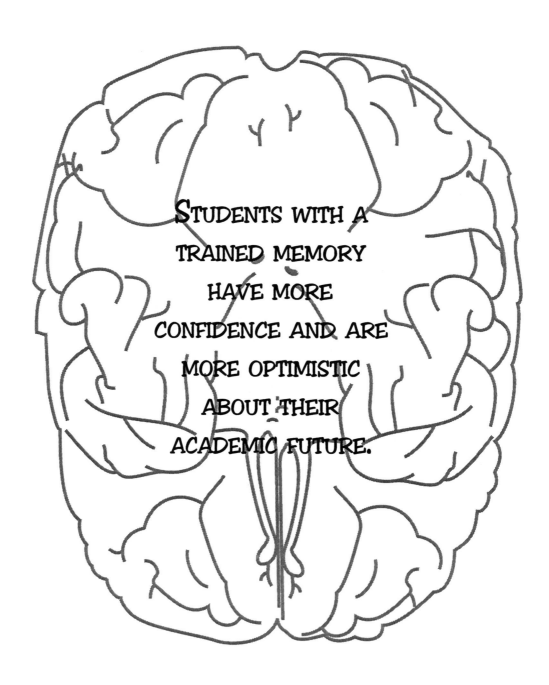

STUDENTS WITH A
TRAINED MEMORY
HAVE MORE
CONFIDENCE AND ARE
MORE OPTIMISTIC
ABOUT THEIR
ACADEMIC FUTURE.

to remember.

T ⇨ **Tunes**

Tunes can be a powerful way to bring back memory, and to facilitate learning. Dr. Giorgi Lozanov (Meier, 2000), the father of accelerated learning, discovered that by playing music, such as Baroque music, at 60 beats per minute, the brain can absorb large amounts of data in a relaxed and easy way. One powerful way to do this is to use some Baroque music, and then pulse information in four-second chunks. For example, "The word 'bonjour' means 'hello' ", pause, one two three four. The beauty of this system is that students can be learning during "non-learning" time, such as in lineups, or while travelling on the bus.

> *Action:* Model a lesson of using music to remember information in the classroom. Encourage students to develop their own memory tapes.

Congratulations!

You now have access to nineteen powerful tools for boosting retention and recall in the classroom. Begin by using the tools you feel most comfortable with, and expand your repertoire from there.

Remember . . .

To boost students' retention and recall, just remember to SAVE, and that STAR TEACHERS GO FOR IT.

Chapter 6

BrainSMART

BARCODE For

The BRAIN:

Read the

7 S.T.R.I.P.E.S. of the

Learning Brain

145

EVERY BRAIN IS AS UNIQUE AS A FINGERPRINT. EVERY STUDENT HAS THEIR OWN BEST WAY OF LEARNING.

AS YOU READ THE BARCODE FOR THE BRAIN, WE SUGGEST REFLECTING ON THESE 2 THINGS:

➲ WHERE ARE YOU ON THE CONTINUUM OF EACH OF THE STRIPES?

➲ WHERE ARE YOUR STUDENTS ON EACH OF THE STRIPES?

Introduction to the Concept of Learning Style – Personality Style

Would you like to reach all of the learners in your classroom? What would it be like if we could better understand and communicate successfully with our family members, friends, and coworkers more often? For the past 25 years educators it has been common practice to consider students' learning styles as an important consideration in schools and classrooms.

Historically, many of the frameworks for considering learning styles, however, came from the work of Carl Jung (1971) in his exploration of different *personality types* that began to be published in the 1920s. The similarities to Jung's seminal work in the field of psychology are most easily seen with various assessment instruments that consider basically four different ways of seeing and experiencing the world. The Barcode of the Brain: 7 S.T.R.I.P.E.S. of the Learning Brain is another way of looking at the personality of learners in ways that might be new to you.

As we have taught both young people and adults for many years, we have developed the Barcode of the Brain: 7 S.T.R.I.P.E.S. of the Learning Brain Model. The characteristics that comprise the model are aspects of personality that appear over and over to make a difference in the classroom. When they go unnoticed we have seen great problems occur! When they are affirmed, often students (and participants in workshops) learn easier!

As you read this chapter consider, if you will, the following five key issues: First, each pair of characteristics, for example, Sameness- Difference, should be considered as being at two ends of a continuum. That is, Sameness is at one end, and Difference is at the other end. Further, consider that all people, children through adult, are somewhere on the continuum and never on the very furthermost point at either end. Although, we do concede that often those with whom we have trouble communicating often seem to be at the very end of the continuum!

Second, we believe that while brains tend to be wired for being toward one end of the continuum or the other, experiences in life give us opportunities to grow in the other direction on the continuum as well. These experiences also give us a chance to develop greater consciousness about ourselves too. So, in a nutshell, as life comes along, we may change on this scale as we make use of experiences.

Third, these aspects of personality are both learnable and teachable, we usually say "coachable." In fact, you will notice in our comments about courageous learners that students who have difficulty in school often have

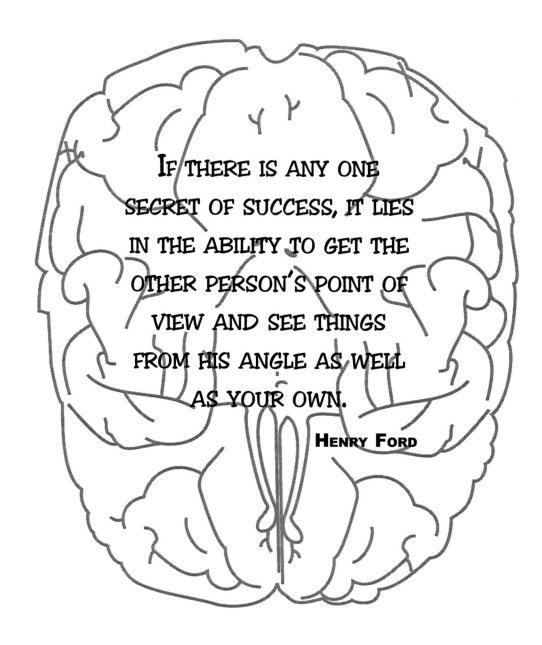

IF THERE IS ANY ONE
SECRET OF SUCCESS, IT LIES
IN THE ABILITY TO GET THE
OTHER PERSON'S POINT OF
VIEW AND SEE THINGS
FROM HIS ANGLE AS WELL
AS YOUR OWN.

HENRY FORD

STRATEGIES FOR REACHING STUDENTS WHO LIKE SAMENESS INCLUDE HAVING IN A MORNING SONG, SUCCESS RITUALS, REGULAR TIME FOR STORIES OR SHARING. WHAT ELSE COULD YOU DO?

STRATEGIES FOR STUDENTS WHO PREFER DIFFERENCE INCLUDE BRINGING IN A MYSTERY OBJECT, HAVING GUEST SPEAKERS OR TEACHING STUDENTS A RANGE OF DIFFERENT PROBLEM SOLVING STRATEGIES. WHAT ELSE DO YOU DO TO BRING DIFFERENCE INTO YOUR CLASSROOM?

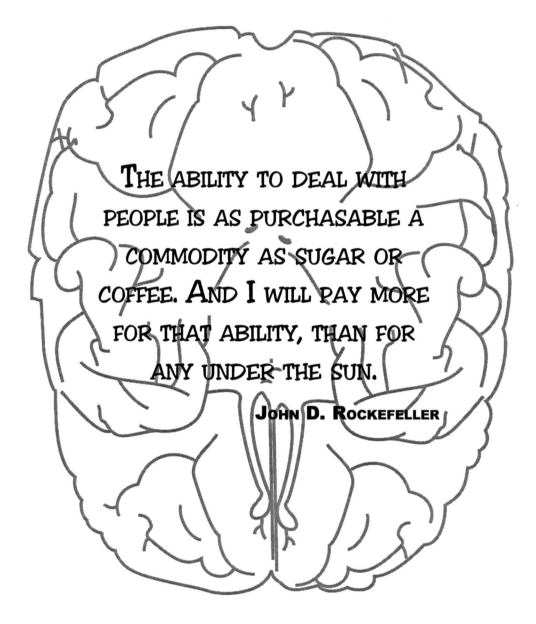

THE ABILITY TO DEAL WITH PEOPLE IS AS PURCHASABLE A COMMODITY AS SUGAR OR COFFEE. AND I WILL PAY MORE FOR THAT ABILITY, THAN FOR ANY UNDER THE SUN.

JOHN D. ROCKEFELLER

habits that cause them trouble each day. One very important way that teachers have used this model is to coach courageous learners in how to become more flexible in their thinking so that they can more be successful toward the end of the continuum where they have trouble. For example, to take the before mentioned example, many courageous learners that we know are very Difference code and need to be coached in ways to understand, respect, and function well when things are more toward the Sameness code.

Fourth, many studies in education state that the skill of thinking about one's own thinking, also called metacognition, is the "Number 1" characteristic of students that make them successful in school and life. In terms of the Barcode of the Brain, this important research means that students must be able to think about their own code and how they can use it, develop flexibility around it, and use the code for successful communication with others.

Lastly, and importantly, use the Barcode of the Brain: Seven Stripes of the Learning Brain to have fun in your classrooms and life, as you encourage you students to do the same. We have fun teaching it and teachers that we work with do too!

Sameness – Difference

People with more of a "sameness" code prefer to go to the same places, do the same things, and are uncomfortable with change. They often reframe new information to fit with their existing mindset. Whereas, people who prefer difference enjoy different experiences, doing new things, and often look to discover ways to positively change their lives.

How does the sameness – difference factor affect courageous learners?

First, many courageous learners have a strong "difference" code. They learn best given choices about their learning whenever possible. They also often appreciate having a chance to have a voice when they have something to contribute that is different from others in class.

Second, while courageous learners often appreciate difference more than sameness, many benefit from positive rituals that give a sense of predictability. For example, starting class on time every day. Another way to honor this need is to map out the school year at a ceremony at the beginning of the year and let the graduates from the previous year lead students through the map that illustrates exciting elements of the coming year.

Third, many courageous learners need specific training in cognitive flexibility, or flexible thinking. This need is illustrated by the fact that often

GETTING STUDENTS TO WRITE GOALS, GIVING POSITIVE FEED BACK, AND TELLING SUCCESS STORIES ABOUT OTHER STUDENTS YOU HAVE WORKED WITH CAN APPEAL TO THE TOWARDS CODE.

WHAT ELSE COULD YOU DO?

they continue to do the same things that do not work well. For example, when they feel they are provoked, many students only see one option, to fight. They often get a reputation of "bully." Others see only one option, and that is to flee, or duck. These are often the "victims." Both have serious consequences and are the result of inflexible thinking. Coaching for flexible thinking is important for these students and includes questioning, "What might have been other options for you?" Also, "How can you keep from setting yourself up?" is another important question for thinking coaches to ask courageous learners.

Fourth, courageous learners often have difficulty with transitions, such as passing time in the halls, standing in line for lunch, and the time before school begins. While transition times are necessary for the difference they often crave, until they have coaching in how to "do transitions," they often get into trouble. Two very important aspects of coaching for this problem are handling time and space. See the BrainSMART Tools for Thinking chapter for more information on coaching these two aspects of thinking.

Actions that affirm both styles

- Have silent reading enjoyment hour at the same time every day. For example, teachers who we've worked with in NYC Community District six have *The Golden Hour* for silent reading.

- Give students choice so that they can decide what they read.

- With important literary works have all students read the same book and give them choice about which character they can "act out."

- After students read a story give them a choice about how they are assessed.

- Have social or play time at the same time each day and offer different possibilities for enjoying the time.

A question to ask yourself to better understand where you are on the sameness – difference continuum is as follows. "How does what you did last year compare to what you did the year before?"

Towards – Away

Those who have more of a "moving towards" code focus more on moving towards their goals, tend to be optimistic, and often have difficulty seeing obstacles. People with more of a moving away from code are good at seeing risks and obstacles and focus on avoiding problems. They may be slightly more pessimistic.

PLAYING MUSIC AND CREATING TIME DURING THE DAY FOR STUDENTS TO MOVE ARE GREAT IDEAS FOR STUDENTS WHO NEED A LOT OF SENSORY STIMULATION IN THEIR DAY. WHAT ARE YOUR IDEAS FOR POSITIVE STIMULATION IN THE CLASSROOM?

SOME TEACHERS USE SCENT IN THE CLASSROOM SO THAT STUDENTS RECEIVE POSITIVE SENSORY STIMULATION FROM SMELLS SUCH AS LEMON AND PEPPERMINT.

Actions that affirm both styles

- Give students many opportunities to have new learning experiences to validate "towards behavior."

- Create a trusting learning environment where minimal risk is experienced as learning occurs.

- Create a classroom environment where mistakes are a natural part of the learning process.

How does the towards – away factor affect courageous learners?

Often courageous learners begin their life journey by taking positive steps, literally, toward those they love. Then, with many children, difficulties happen and they begin to do one of two things. They either continue to move toward and try at school, or they quit taking the risks to learn because of a fear of failure. For both groups, it is important to teach them how to read cues to determine if they are moving forward in positive ways. For example, when speaking, students must be able to ascertain if others can understand what they are attempting to communicate. Good thinking coaches ask, "What are the cues?" Often courageous learners do not understand that there are cues, and that they can learn to read them. Cues make it possible for these students to successfully "move toward" when appropriate and know when to proceed with caution.

Second, it is very important to note that courageous learners often appear to be interested in moving away in most every circumstance. However, this is not often what they deeply want and need. They have often developed this stance as a way to protect themselves from fear of failure, because they have a history of failure at school and/or in life. Often a kind word, a pat on the back, and coaching for success help to get these students moving toward their goals.

A question to ask yourself to better understand where you are on the towards – away from continuum is as follows. "Why did you choose your current job?"

Resistance Need High– Need for Little Resistance

Children and youth with a high resistance need tend to enjoy a large amount of stimulation (Ayers, 1972). The stimulation they seek may be auditory. For example, students who enjoy very loud music, fireworks, movies and other auditory experiences illustrate this type of resistance. Many students today seek large amounts of kinesthetic stimulation. For example, touch and food are examples of kinesthetic stimulation. Often people with high

BE THE LEARNER
YOU WANT YOUR
STUDENTS TO
BECOME.

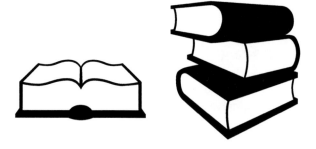

resistance needs get into trouble at home, school, and even with the law unless they learn how to deal with these needs.

People with a need for little resistance do not enjoy great amounts of stimulation, and, in fact, are often quite bothered by it. For example, a second grade boy who author Donna taught appeared to become angry each day as class began and ended. As we investigated what the problem might be, we found that he had a very low need for auditory resistance. Therefore, the ringing of the bell (he sat under it) hurt his ears and he became upset. All he needed was to be moved from under the bell to cut the auditory resistance he received from the bell. The child who has a low tolerance for touch is one who has a need for little kinesthetic resistance. It is very bothersome for these children to be touched, kicked, or hit by those who are looking for resistance in this way.

Actions that affirm both styles

- Notice individual differences on the resistance continuum and intervene when necessary to change the learning environment for children/youth

- Coach both high resistance and low resistance learners about this in themselves and others

- Offer some high resistance learning activities such as movement and music

- Also have low resistance learning activities such as silent reading and reflection

- Vary high and low resistance activities throughout the day

How does the towards – away factor affect courageous learners?

First, many courageous learners are high resistance learners. They often appear to be the loudest, and they tend to move around a lot. Both behaviors often get them into trouble at school. For these students, structured movement is very important throughout the day. We recommend brainobics. Brainobics are exercises that allow students to cross the midline of the body with enjoyable movements to help them learn. For many courageous learners, movement may be the difference in whether they learn at school or not. Music is also a great way to reach high resistance learners in the classroom, as it provides auditory resistance. We present specific brainobics in our book *BrainSMART Strategies for Boosting Test Scores* (2000).

157

TIME IS ONE OF THE MOST ABSTRACT CONCEPTS, AND IT IS IMPORTANT TO CONSIDER IT A SERIOUS UNIT OF STUDY FOR CHILDREN AND YOUTH.

GIVE STUDENTS MANY TIMES TO EXPERIMENT WITH TIMING THEMSELVES BEFORE TEST TIME. IT OFTEN HAPPENS THAT STUDENTS ARE PUNISHED ON TESTING BECAUSE THEY HAVE BEEN STUCK ON ONE PROBLEM AND NOT MOVED TO PROBLEMS THEY COULD WORK.

Second, courageous learners need to develop self awareness about their need for resistance. High resistance learners need to know this about themselves so that they can channel it properly. For example, learners with a high need for kinesthetic resistance can get this resistance and develop self discipline through sports like tennis, rowing, tai chi, and walking.

Third, we should not underestimate the importance of this continuum in education and caregiving. Children and youth at both ends of this continuum often become "somewhat of a mystery" to adults around them. Often those who need a great amount of resistance tend to upset adults, and we attribute "willfulness" to their behavior. In fact, with young children often they do not know that their loud voice or hard hits are abnormal. They think that the world and everyone in it has a brain body system like theirs! That is until they have a caring long-term intervention in place where they can receive caring and corrective feedback.

Children, and particularly babies with their parents, who have a very low tolerance for tactile stimulation often make their parents feel very inadequate when they cry when held. Parents and teachers need to be assured that this is a brain body issue that they did not create through their behavior.

A question to ask yourself to better understand where you are on the resistance continuum is as follows. "Do I like a lot of sensory stimulation in my life on a daily basis?"

In Time – Through Time

People with more of an "in time" code tend to live in the moment, give full attention to the present task, and are less concerned about what time it is. Whereas, people with a more "through time" code are great at planning their time and will often be focused on the next task or a meeting that is coming up.

Actions that affirm both styles

- Coach students in the importance of planning and how to plan.

- Offer students "in time" opportunities for free time where they can construct experiences from appropriate materials and centers.

- Coach students to be aware of when it is important to be in "through time" and when it's great to "stop and smell the roses."

159

THE PERCEPTION OF OPTIONS
AND CHOICE IN THE
LEARNING PROCESS CAN
INCREASE MOTIVATION AND
PERSISTENCE.

How does the in time – through time factor affect courageous learners?

Courageous learners often have a very difficult time with this factor. How many courageous learners have you known that appear to know only "in time?" This is a problem for them in life, for example, in secondary school as they begin to apply for jobs. They are often even late for the interview! On tests, learners of all ages are often punished greatly for not spending the proper amount of time per item. It is important for courageous learners to be coached so that they can be successful in the U.S. culture that is more "through time."

For courageous learners to be successful, they must develop an understanding of time as it relates to school. Time is only learned through coaching and is very culturally dependent. For example, students come to school with very diverse understanding of time. If their home culture "chunks" time in large units, such as morning, afternoon, and evening, so will they. Further, if this is the case, students will often appear very late, or early, in terms of the way school culture uses time. If, at home, it is acceptable to arrive any time during the morning, then the child will think the same is true at school. Often both parents and students benefit from coaching that is non-judgmental about time.

A question to ask yourself to better understand where you are on the "in time – through time" continuum is as follows. For an eight o'clock meeting what time would you usually arrive?

Procedures – Options

People with a strong "procedural" code like most things in their lives to have a beginning, middle, and an end. They like to have a specific sequence of steps. Whereas, people with a strong "options" code do not like to use other people's procedures. They prefer to create their own. They love options and variety.

Actions that affirm both styles

- Occasionally give students options for the method of assessment over their learning.

- Allow students to have input into operating procedures within the classroom when possible.

- Make classroom procedures clear in all modalities so that all may follow them.

161

TEACHING BARCODE FOR THE BRAIN HELPS OUR STUDENTS BECOME BOTH MORE REFLECTIVE ABOUT THEMSELVES (INTERNAL) AND MORE ABLE TO HAVE A TRUE UNDERSTANDING OF OTHERS (EXTERNAL).

JOURNALING IS A GREAT WAY TO HELP STUDENTS CONNECT WITH THEIR WRITING IN A HEART FELT WAY.

- Give students options in learning, for example, by using different learning centers.

How does the procedures - options factor affect courageous learners?

Most courageous learners are more toward "options" on this continuum, and we have found most classrooms to be more procedural. So, it is best to give courageous learners options whenever possible.

Some courageous learners have difficulty performing a sequence of operations. In fact, many have more difficulty with a procedural sequence than they would creating a brand new process for doing something. So, make sure that courageous learners understand how to perform the required procedures before assuming they do.

A question to ask yourself to better understand where you are on the procedures and options continuum is as follows. "Do I use a lot of procedures to keep life running smoothly, or do I like to keep my options open as much as possible?"

External – Internal

People with a more external code are good at reading other people's views and feelings and tend to be keen to gather a great deal of external information when making decisions. More internal people are less interested in other's views or external data and make up their minds based on their own direct experiences.

Actions that affirm both styles

- Offer many chances for students to come up with their best way to solve a problem, for example, in mathematics calculations (internal code).

- Allow students time for writing in reflective journals so they have time to internalize their own experiences of learning.

- Give ample, timely, and constructive external feedback on samples of student work.

How does the external – internal factor affect courageous learners?

Many courageous learners are internally driven. The often heard statement, " Oh, she just marches to her own drummer" is a way many teachers and

To be effective as a teacher we must always connect the specifics to the big picture. This helps us reach courageous learners!

The brain learns best when it sees the big picture first and is able to connect specific details in a meaningful pattern.

parents often characterize these learners. Affirmation of positive and creative acts that come from this factor are often very powerful for courageous learners.

When learning something that is difficult for them, courageous learners need to have feedback quickly and often so that they do not fall into a habit of incorrect problem solving. After a topic has been introduced, computer generated feedback is a great way for courageous learners to get a great deal of quick feedback and still "save face" with the teacher and peers when the computer informs them they have made a mistake.

Given that courageous learners come into our classrooms with a long history of failure, they are often not so happy about receiving external input. When working with courageous learners, look to find something good about them, or what they have done.

A question to ask yourself to better understand where you are on the external - internal continuum is as follows. "How do you know that you're doing a good job?"

Specifics – Big Picture

People with a more "specifics" code focus on details and specifics. They are great at spotting errors in detail. Whereas, people with a stronger "big picture" code are focused on the big picture and how important aspects of life connect together. They are often less interested in details and specifics.

Actions that affirm both styles

- When students work in groups, when appropriate, assign a detail person to edit the project. Rotate the position.

- When students read, check to see if they understand the main ideas in the story.

- Let students joyfully "catch the teacher" when making a mistake, for example, as you model the working of a math problem on the board.

- Allow students time to construct mandalas to guide them as they learn to construct wholes.

- Coach students to be able to sort relevant from irrelevant information when problem solving.

EVERY HUMAN BEING IS AS UNIQUE AS A FINGERPRINT.

How does the specifics – big picture factor affect courageous learners?

Often courageous learners do very well when they solve familiar problems such as those found in their lives. At school, however, when students might not be familiar with the school experience, they are apt to have difficulty constructing a "big picture" that results in a good grade. For example, both authors have known students who are actually financially supporting their families while they are in high school. These students organize their finances at a high level of analysis so that the families can survive month to month. However, when it comes to being able to organize an essay, they need specific coaching to bridge the skill of organizing (in finances) to organizing an essay in English class.

In classwork, homework, and test taking, many courageous learners often spend a great amount of time "stuck" on one problem instead of moving on to finalize the others. This is particularly important on tests that are timed. Students should be coached to not stay "stuck" on one problem, but to move on and solve others.

A question to ask yourself to better understand where you are on the procedures and options continuum is as follows. "Are you a good proofreader, or editor?"

"What is your life mission?"

Key Considerations:

1. **Every human being is as unique as a fingerprint.**

2. **Our stripes will change from context to context.**

3. **Two or three codes tend to be our prominent motivators.**

167

Chapter 7

Inspiring Examples: Stories From State and District Initiatives

169

OUR EDUCATIONAL SYSTEM FAVORS STUDENTS THAT CAN PROCESS LINEARLY, TAKE INFORMATION AUDITORIALLY AND VISUALLY, LOOK AT THE TEACHER, AND RESTATE PIECES OF INFORMATION IN A LOGICAL, LINEAR FASHION. IN STUDIES THESE STUDENTS ARE LISTED AS FULL SENSORY ACCESS. STUDIES SHOW THEY MAKE UP, ON AVERAGE, ONLY 15% OF THE TEST POPULATION.

ADAPTED FROM HANNAFORD (1995)

The S.T.A.R. Story

"Our Math Scores went up 20 Points!"

Steve Hawes

1999 BrainSMART S.T.A.R. Cadre

State of Florida Dropout Prevention Initiative

As mentioned before, we believe that teaching is applied neuroscience and that all teachers deserve the training tools, time, and compensation for such a noble and important profession. Steve Hawes, one of the cadre of the 1999 BrainSMART S.T.A.R. program, was thrilled to see how his students' test scores went up after applying the BrainSMART strategies in the classroom. Another participant, Angel Cole, was named teacher of the year as reviewers observed her using BrainSMART strategies in the classroom with her students. (Test scores of the students have gone up approximately 38% in the last three years.)

Much more important to us is that our cadre consistently switched on the level of learning and built the practical optimism that fuels lifelong success in school and in life. It was inspiring for us to see Steve, Angel, and other members of the cadre really making a difference in the life of their students as we visited the classrooms across Florida.

The BrainSMART S.T.A.R. program began as a journey with an idea at *The Brain, the Mind, and the Learner* conference at Lake Tahoe in 1998. Here leading neuroscientists and educators, who apply brain research, met at a conference designed to equip participants with tools, techniques, and further knowledge by improving academic success by all students. At the conference, a dynamic trio from Florida hatched their plan. Mary Jo Butler from the Florida Department of Education, Dr. Lola Heverly, an educational consultant, and Dr. Nancy Romain from the Department of Education Drop-Out Prevention program.

Author Marcus was one of the keynote speakers at this conference. As the dynamic trio began to talk to author Marcus, they began to see fabulous possibilities for launching statewide what is the world's first systematic application of brain research helping students at risk. Drawing on research that supports effective professional development, the team decided to arrange a five-day BrainSMART summer workshop for a cadre of teachers who would have positions within the school that directly influence the lives of students at risk of academic failure. The teachers would come in pairs so that, through the

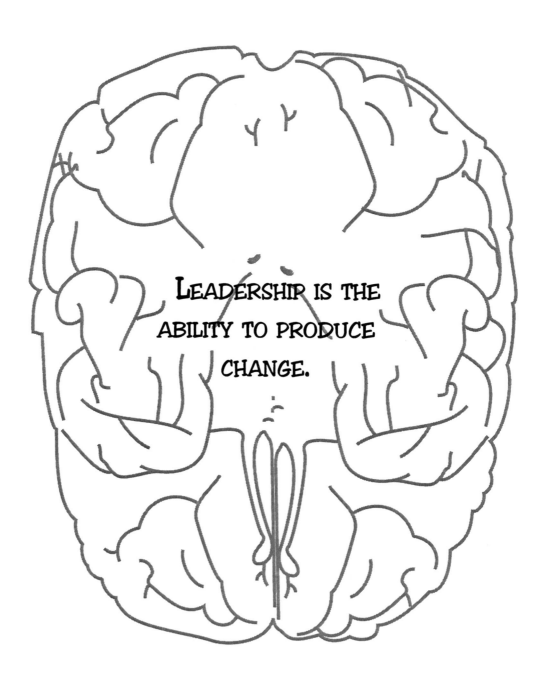

LEADERSHIP IS THE ABILITY TO PRODUCE CHANGE.

buddy system, they could support one another's success after the five day training.

In alignment with the National Staff Development Council's guidelines, it was decided to follow up the five day workshop with four follow workshops where other leading educators could add to the knowledge base of our cadre of teachers. The third and final stage was that Marcus "The Brain Guy" and author Donna "Dr. Donna" would visit the schools to witness first hand the wonderful work of the teachers and to model some strategies with the students. The idea was a great one and at the time of writing, we are now moving to recruit the third cadre as the third year of this powerful project unfolds.

Perhaps the most exciting thing about the S.T.A.R. process is that the teachers went through a personal and professional transformation as they went through the process of learning and teaching. Importantly, the first five-day workshop allowed the S.T.A.R. teachers to have a rich, deep, and transforming experience as they learn the BrainSMART way. Each teacher created a strong bond and network with others who could help sustain effort as each teacher went back to apply what they learned in the classroom. The four follow up workshops allowed time for reflecting on what was working for them and what was needed for further improvement. They also added to their knowledge and skill base as outside speakers such as our friend and colleague Bob Sylwester, Ph.D., and Jerome Morton, Ph.D., joined us for two of the follow up workshops.

As part of the project, the S.T.A.R. cadre members completed mind maps of what they learned from the BrainSMART training and put together examples of BrainSMART strategies that they used in the classrooms. This idea allows us to build an ever-expanding BrainSMART toolbox of effective strategies that teachers have actually used in the classroom to help their students become more successful. The teachers enjoyed the process as they shared ideas and multiplied their tools!

As we are writing this book we are in the process of reviewing the early results of our first year of the S.T.A.R. process. It seems clear that all the participants gained significant knowledge, skills, and strategies. Stories such as Steve's and Angel's indicate there has also been an increase in test scores. Another major goal of the S.T.A.R. project was to insure that after we trained the original cadre, these teacher leaders would inspire others to be curious about the BrainSMART process. Once again, we were pleased with the early results of the effort.

STAR TEACHERS SEEK TO
ESTABLISH IN-DEPTH CARING
RELATIONSHIPS IN THE COURSE OF
DAY-TO-DAY TEACHING ACTIVITIES,
AND TO AVOID, DEFLECT, OR DEFUSE
PROBLEMS THAT WOULD INEVITABLY
ARISE IF SUCH RAPPORT HAD NOT
BEEN DEVELOPED.

In Nassau County, authors Donna and Marcus did a workshop for four districts. S.T.A.R. cadre member Lynne Gelinas's work in Brevard County has developed a high level of interest, and when combined with a visit by author Marcus "The Brain Guy," a district wide professional development day was devoted to BrainSMART. We will follow up here with more training. In Monroe County, the S.T.A.R. project has resulted in a high level of district wide support for a five-day cadre training in August of 2000. Furthermore, in addition to other workshops throughout the Keys, authors Marcus and Donna will be placing online many of their top strategies from the workshop to ensure sustained support for the cadre.

To date we have learned many things from this process. *First*, give teacher leaders a solid five day transformational experience, so that they can begin to internalize the BrainSMART process to boost student achievement. Ensure that the teachers enjoy the process so they become fully engaged and excited about what they have learned when they get back in their classrooms. *Second*, sustain the support with follow-up meetings throughout the year to keep momentum going and sustain a fresh exchange of ideas about what is working well. Furthermore, the visits by Marcus "The Brain Guy" and "Dr. Donna" help bring the message home to schools where the teachers applied the strategies they had learned. *Third*, keep it practical. One of the most consistent pieces of feedback we received throughout this process is how *practical* the strategies are, and that teachers apply them and see positive results with their students. At the same time, the teachers agree that it is important for us to connect practical applications with a strong *scientific background* from brain and cognitive research. Thus, the research to practice built confidence behind what the teachers were doing. They had an ability to explain why they were doing what they were doing. *Fourth*, the process needs high-level administrative support.

We were fortunate to have Mary Jo Butler from Florida Department of Education supporting this process from her senior position. Dr. Nancy Romain put considerable energy into sustaining the process throughout the year, and Dr. Lola Heverly was a powerful source for insuring that the Pre-K members of the S.T.A.R. cadre got the support they needed to be successful.

Summary

This fledgling process seems to show great promise. Time will tell if we can sustain the momentum that has moved the project along so far. What is clear is that teachers can make a great difference in the lives of courageous learners when their wisdom and compassion are combined with better understanding of the science of learning and assisting the strategies for helping all students be successful.

IF EXPERIENCE, RESEARCH, AND COMMON SENSE TEACH NOTHING ELSE, THEY CONFIRM THE TRUISM THAT PEOPLE LEARN AT DIFFERENT RATES, AND IN DIFFERENT WAYS WITH DIFFERENT SUBJECTS.

A District's Story: Meeting the Needs of Courageous Learners

Translating common sense and research into practice

As we meet educators around the U.S. who are working with at-risk learners, we marvel at the creative and innovative ways they are working to meet the needs of these learners. One powerful example is illustrated from author Donna's practice as a teacher and school psychologist in Norman, Oklahoma. This story is told in honor of the students and educators who are a part of the story.

At the time of this project, Donna, a practicing school psychologist, had provided diagnostic evaluations for over 1000 students who were referred by their teachers as candidates for special education services. From Donna's vantage point it became very clear that greater energy needed to be put into prevention and intervention efforts for at-risk learners. The specific changes that Donna saw as necessary for over 95% of the students that she assessed were methods that give at-risk students the thinking and learning skills they need for success.

Our story (Wilson & Church, 1993) shows how one school district bravely examined the problem of growing numbers of special education referrals, too few interventions for at-risk learners, fragmentation of services, and obtaining more school psychologists as well as changing the method of delivery of school psychological services.

OVERVIEW OF TASK FORCE

The written purpose for organizing the At-Risk Task Force was fourfold:

1) To obtain a clear and thorough understanding of the current situation of at-risk learners in the community,

2) To review and select the most effective and innovative practices for supporting students at-risk in achieving academic success,

3) To systematically implement these best practices in a coherent way, and

4) To identify and obtain models which would better integrate Special Education, Regular Education, and At-Risk programs.

"IT WAS IMPORTANT TO ME TO BE ABLE TO SHARE IDEAS WITH COLLEAGUES ON THE TASK FORCE. WE OFTEN SPOKE OF THE SCHOOL PSYCHOLOGISTS' ROLE WITH AT-RISK STUDENTS. IT SEEMED TO TRANSFORM OTHERS VIEW OF WHAT PSYCHOLOGISTS CAN PROVIDE ALL STUDENTS."

DONNA WILSON, PH.D.

To determine which of the many innovative programs were appropriate for the district, it was necessary to investigate the Special Education and other At-Risk programs, which our district currently has in place. It was also necessary to thoroughly examine the research on these issues and to identify and study any related model programs. In order to complete these investigations, the Task Force was divided into four committees. Given the unique and important viewpoint of the school psychologists, each of the four committees was chaired by a school psychologist from the Special Services Department.

The Committees met independently and often. Committee members worked individually or in small groups, depending on the chosen task. Each month the committees met jointly. These monthly Task Force meetings were scheduled as information and business meetings. It was during these meetings that committees reported their progress and made decisions regarding the on-going activities of the Task Force.

The At-Risk Task Force included representation from all areas of certified staff. It was a true cross-section of the Norman Public Schools including teachers from Regular Education, Special Education, and Gifted Education, Counselors, Principals, Assistant Principals, Speech Pathologists, and Directors. Certified staff from local state schools for special needs students were also included. Both elementary and secondary were represented. This was considered important as often services for at-risk students appear fragmented.

Very early in the study, the Task Force members adopted the Levels of Prevention Model as a method of organizing At-Risk Programs in the Norman Public Schools. The adoption of this model changed the direction of the Task Force. It became apparent that Special Education was at one end of an At-Risk continuum rather than a separate and distinct program that stands alone. Again, the purpose for using such a model was to decrease fragmentation of services, and begin to further conceptualize the need for prevention of learner difficulties. At this time the name of the Task Force changed from the Special Education At-Risk Task Force to the At-Risk Task Force. The Levels of Prevention Model is represented with examples on page 189:

AT-RISK COMMITTEE

The At-Risk Committee reviewed and revised the list of concerns generated by the Task Force chairmen. The Committee developed a paradigm to collect information describing the At-Risk Programs in the Norman Public

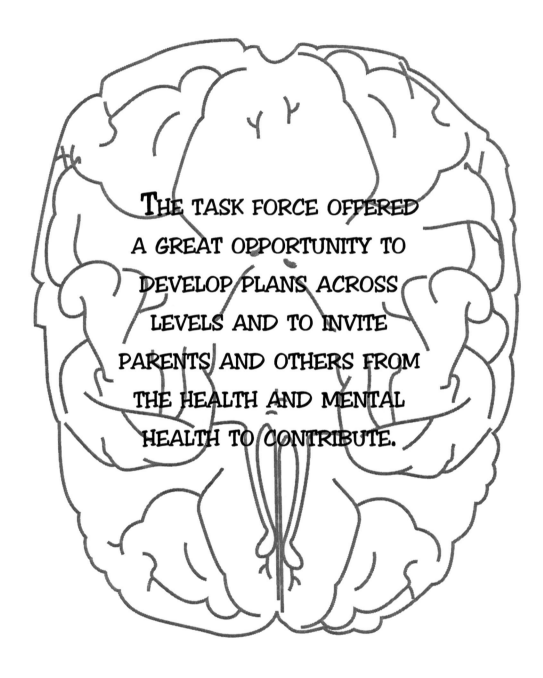

THE TASK FORCE OFFERED
A GREAT OPPORTUNITY TO
DEVELOP PLANS ACROSS
LEVELS AND TO INVITE
PARENTS AND OTHERS FROM
THE HEALTH AND MENTAL
HEALTH TO CONTRIBUTE.

"The world has changed and the schools haven't."

—Bruce Goldberg, Center for Restructuring

ISSUES EFFECTING EDUCATION

➤ 90% of new jobs are in the service & information industries.

➤ Some neurobiologists believe that 100% of the U.S. population is at-risk for stress related problems.

➤ 4% of children live in traditional families.

➤ 25% of children live in single parent homes.

➤ 25% of the population lives in poverty.

➤ 50% of children with parents under age 25 live in poverty.

➤ 20% unemployment rate at ages 20 - 24

➤ By the year 2020 depression will be the leading cause of illness in the U.S.

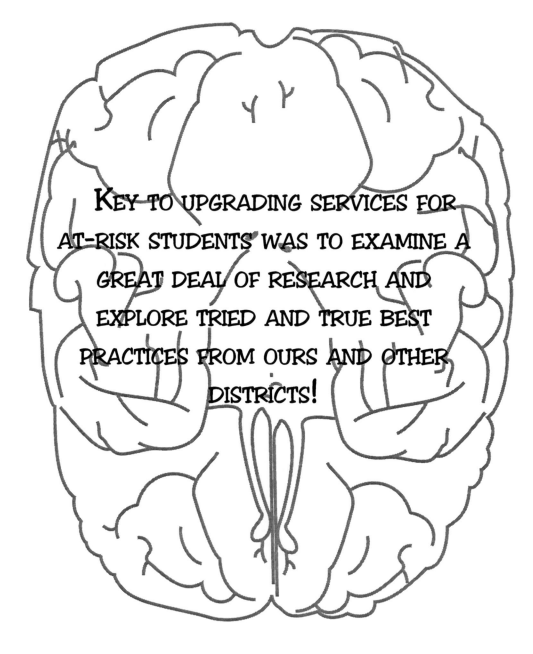

Key to upgrading services for at-risk students was to examine a great deal of research and explore tried and true best practices from ours and other districts!

Levels of Prevention Service Delivery

I. Primary Intervention
    A. Strengthens the well-being of individuals
    B. Is available to the entire population
    C. Available to students not yet identified as having a problem
    D. Is a proactive stance
    E. Examples are:
        1. Affective education programs
        2. Social skills programs
        3. Study skills programs
        4. WHO, Say It Straight, Just Say No

II. Secondary Prevention
    A. Services are available to a select group at high risk for problems.
        1. Students who are members of a high risk group
        2. Students who manifest early signs of a later dysfunction
    B. Primary Prevention did not prove adequate
    C. Requires identification of At-Risk factors
    D. Examples are:
        1. Dropout Prevention programs
        2. Divorce Counseling groups
        3. Academic tutoring
        4. Counseling

III. Tertiary Prevention (Remediation and Rehabilitation)
    A. Intervention after a negative outcome has occurred (Failure is identified)
    B. Seeks to reduce residual effects or adverse consequences of a disorder or failure
    C. Requires documentation of failure to access services
    D. Labels are applied to the student
    E. Examples are:
        1. Special Education
        2. Alternative schools

183

As part of our discussion about children with ADD, the school psychologists hosted a meeting with a respected pediatrician, concerned parents, and a host of educators so that concerns could be aired, information shared, and plans made.

DONNA WILSON, PH.D.

Schools (Wilson & Church, 1993). During the first phase, each Committee member interviewed two or more principals to gather the following information.

1) What is the definition of "At-Risk student" in your building?

2) How does the staff in your building identify At-Risk students?

3) List each program offered in your building to assist At-Risk students.

4) What is the program's purpose?

5) How are the outcomes of each program evaluated?

Issues of Concern for the Task Force as a Whole

1) Fragmentation of services

2) Students "falling through the cracks" if they did not qualify for special education services

3) Need for thinking and learning programs for at-risk students

4) Need for professional development in learning styles, thinking, and learning skills

5) Need for early childhood prevention education

6) National low employment of special needs students – need for career preparation

7) Need for reorganization of psychological services to include more leadership, prevention, and intervention (to prevent difficulties) along with diagnosis and assessment for possible special education placement after students already exhibited difficulties

The following is the definition for At-Risk students adopted by the At-Risk Task Force:

"The At-Risk student is any student who has the probability for failure in the Norman Public Schools or in his/her community."

RESEARCH AND DEVELOPMENT COMMITTEE

As the investigation of the research literature and model programs began, it became clear that research lead to model programs and model programs were based on research. The two were inextricable. Therefore, the

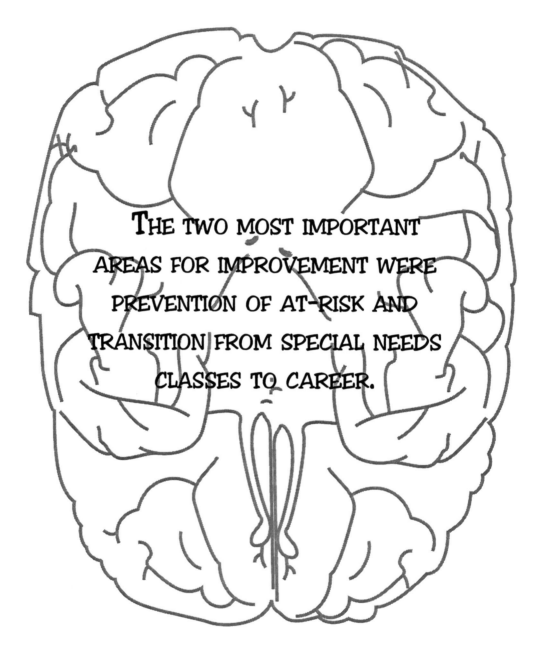

THE TWO MOST IMPORTANT AREAS FOR IMPROVEMENT WERE PREVENTION OF AT-RISK AND TRANSITION FROM SPECIAL NEEDS CLASSES TO CAREER.

Research Committee and the Model Programs committee elected to function in conjunction with one another. The committees used the following format for investigation purposes with committee members selecting the areas for their participation.

I.   Model Programs
    A. Retention
       Transitional
            Chapter 1 & 5
            Title VII
    B. Drug & Alcohol
        Teen Parents
        Dropouts
        Suicide
        Disadvantaged
        Attention Deficit/Hyperactive Disorder
    C. Regular Education Initiative
    D. Special Education Categories
         1. Infant & Preschool Handicapped
         2. Mildly Handicapped
            Learning Disabled & Educable Mentally Handicapped
         3. Moderately & Severely Handicapped
         4. Seriously Emotionally Disturbed/Behavior Disorder
         5. Sensory & Physically Handicapped Other Health Impaired
         6. Speech & Language Impaired
             A. Transition from Secondary Education
             B. Prevocational Programs for At-Risk Special Education
II. Service Delivery Systems
    A. Special Education At-Risk Programs
    B. School Psychology Services
    C. Support Systems for Teachers
    D. Alternative Schools/Programs
III. Organizational Structures

Effective instruction is "hands on" and stimulates higher order thinking. Students taught this way were 70% of a year ahead in science and 40% of a year ahead in math.

The working groups engaged in literature searches using professional journals, computerized data bases and national centers as primary sources of information. A review and critique was written on each investigation and given to the committee chairs. The information was then compiled and shared at the Research and Development Committee meetings. Over 52 model programs and hundreds of research and journal articles were reviewed. As the struggle with the task of organization of such enormous amounts of information unfolded, the committee elected to adopt the Levels of Prevention Model:

LEVELS OF PREVENTION MODEL

Primary Prevention (P-1)

Secondary Prevention (P-2)

Tertiary Prevention (P-3)

It appeared that the greatest needs were in the Primary and Secondary Prevention Levels as well as re-entry from Special Education exclusionary programming to Regular Education inclusionary programming. At this point the focus of the Research & Development Committee became more specifically focused on Prevention Levels 1 (Primary) and 2 (Secondary) and the Blending at the Margins of 3 (Tertiary) between Special Education and Regular Education. The areas of specific investigation then focused on:

Thinking Skills, (P-1 & P-2)

Learning Styles, (P-1 & P-2)

Early Prevention, (P-1 & P-2)

Career Training, (P-1, 2 & 3)

Blending at the Margins, (P-2 & P-3)

Organization, (P-1, 2 & 3)

TASK FORCE RECOMMENDATIONS

The model programs which appeared to best address the needs of Norman students were presented to the Task Force for examination and discussion. After explanation and discussion the Task Force agreed that programs and

SUCCESSFUL TEAMS PLAN TO HAVE CONVERSATIONS ACROSS VARIOUS LEVELS WITHIN THE ORGANIZATION. CHANGE IS BOTH BOTTOM-UP AND TOP-DOWN.

professional development should be recommended for consideration in the six areas named above.

For example, thinking skills programs and professional development were recommended for age levels from kindergarten through high school. Criteria for this area were that the approaches be based on common sense and be well researched; be appealing to students and teachers; and help at-risk students obtain the thinking skills they need for success. The following approaches were chosen because they appeared to meet these criteria.

Courageous Learners: Thinking and Learning

Young Children

The Task Force (Wilson & Church, 1993) identified a cognitive approach developed at the University of Tennessee for students kindergarten through grade 5. The Cognitive Enrichment Network is a program that seeks to apply Feuerstein's theory of Mediated Learning Experience to the classroom environment in the primary grades. The program also includes a parent education component that provides a structured format for helping parents teach their children to be better thinkers and learners.

The Cognitive Enrichment Network program uses ten Building Blocks of Thinking (cognitive functions) to help children learn how to systematically gather information, make a plan for working, and control their expression of thoughts and actions. The Building Blocks of Thinking also help the children to understand why these factors are important in learning. The program also helps children become aware of the need for eight Tools of Independent Learning, which determine one's level of motivation and desire to learn. For example, a mediator using cognitive education helps children develop a feeling of competence by focusing attention on the fact that a child has learned something and how he/she was able to do so. Through this approach, children are encouraged to use behaviors which result in effective learning in different environments. This results in a generalization of these behaviors in a manner which assists children in becoming active and autonomous learners.

Suggestions for mediating the Building Blocks of Thinking and Tools of Independent Learning are provided in 240 Mini Lesson Plans for teachers of first through third graders and 300 Mini Lesson Plans for Kindergarten teachers.

Implementation of each Mini Lesson Plan takes approximately 5 to 20 minutes. Plans for school aged children focus on the need for given Building Blocks and Tools in four types of activities: 1) Initial Instruction 2) Group Practice and Review 3) Instructions for Independent Work and 4) Functional

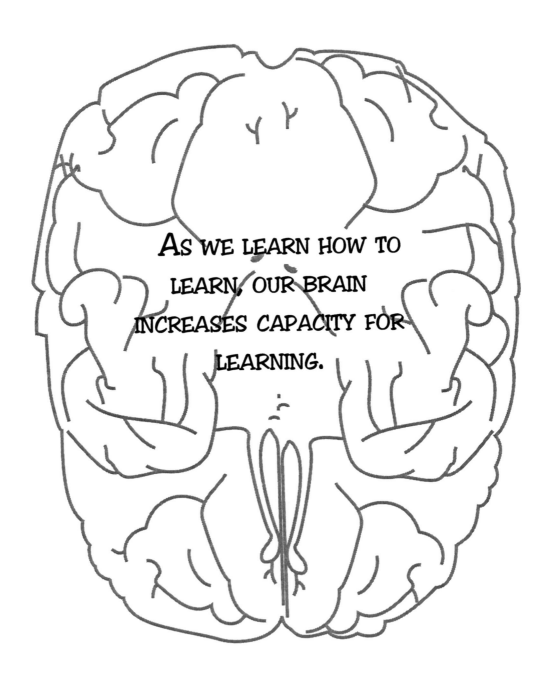

As we learn how to learn, our brain increases capacity for learning.

Living Skills. Plans for Kindergarten focus on: 1) mealtime, 2) art activities, 3) small group activities, and 4) large group activities.

Courageous Learners: Thinking and Learning

Older Children and Youth: Thinking and Learning

For older students, ages 10 through high school, Feuerstein's (1980) Instrumental Enrichment thinking skills/cognitive development program was recommended by the Task Force (Wilson & Church, 1993) as a formal instructional program. It is based on the theories of Cognitive Modifiability and Mediated Learning and is used around the world to help many at-risk students to learn how to learn and think more effectively.

This is a three-year program including 14 instruments or areas of study. Each instrument is divided into units. FIE focuses on the identified areas of cognition through the mediation of the instruments, which introduce the new concept. Together the group identifies the problem, collects information, develops strategies, anticipates possible errors, selects a solution, solves the problem and evaluated the answers.

The students apply the critical thinking process to academic and real life situations. This transfer of learning becomes an habitual model of problem solving and decision making. The classroom discussion is followed by independent problem solving using the FIE exercises. In working through the activities, the students reach mastery of the concepts that have been discussed.

The 14 instruments in the program form a whole that includes the prerequisites for success at school. The Instruments are Organization of Dots. Orientation in Space I, Comparisons, Analytic Perception, Categorization, Family Relations, Temporal Relations, Numerical Progressions, Instructions, Illustrations, Orientation in Space II, Transitive Relations, Syllogisms, and Representational Design. Students not only learn how to think but how to talk about how they think. Most importantly they learn to apply the skills to their lives and at school.

Other Recommendations

After a 3 year study, the Task Force (Wilson & Church, 1993) recommended sixteen programs to serve the needs of the districts' at-risk youth. All were from the six major categories previously mentioned and as follows: Thinking Skills, Learning Styles, Early Prevention, Career Training, Blending at the Margins, and Organization.

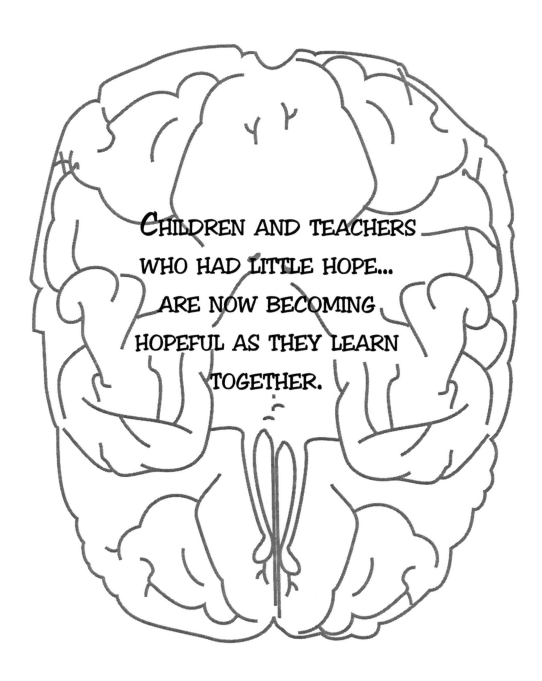

CHILDREN AND TEACHERS
WHO HAD LITTLE HOPE...
ARE NOW BECOMING
HOPEFUL AS THEY LEARN
TOGETHER.

Later the same year the district wrote a grant and received approximately $61,000 for the first-year training of programs at various sites. The plan included the use of thinking skills programs at the elementary and middle school levels. After a successful pilot, the program was expanded through training for a group of 30 teachers, counselors, and psychologists. Additionally, the district began more extensive professional development in the area of learning styles. Two principals each from the elementary and secondary levels became trainers in the 4-MAT system so that the district can continue to build capacity in this area.

As a result of the Task Force, the school psychologists began to serve the district in a different way. Before the Task Force, the four school psychologists rotated through the district serving all 22 school sites. Their primary role was that of diagnostician and intervention specialist. After the Task Force three more school psychology positions were added and each psychologist began to serve a cluster of schools.

Additionally, the school psychologists' roles were expanded to include primary prevention when needed. For example, author Donna joyously served one of her schools by co-teaching for a year in three classes with large numbers of at-risk students. Donna and other school psychologists began to spend more time in teaching and intervening, rather than primarily assessing.

Lastly, as reported in *Research for Better Schools: Thinking and Problem Solving* (Wilson & Church, 1993), the Task Force has altered the way that educators in Norman Public Schools look at the child who is at-risk for learning difficulties. A thinking skills teacher at a district middle school commented that it is exciting to see the children who struggle begin to blossom as they learn impulse control and organizational skills. Children and teachers who had little hope for at-risk childrens' cognitive development are now becoming hopeful as they work together toward higher levels of thinking.

This project illustrates research-based features necessary for changes to be made in schools today. They are as follows:

1) The effort began at the grassroots (with the school psychologists who saw the students in difficulty over and over) and had administrative support,

2) communication went across all certifications and levels (on some occasions parents and university faculty visited as well),

3) regular and special education teachers had lots of communication that enhanced inclusion efforts, as well as prevention, for all at-risk students,

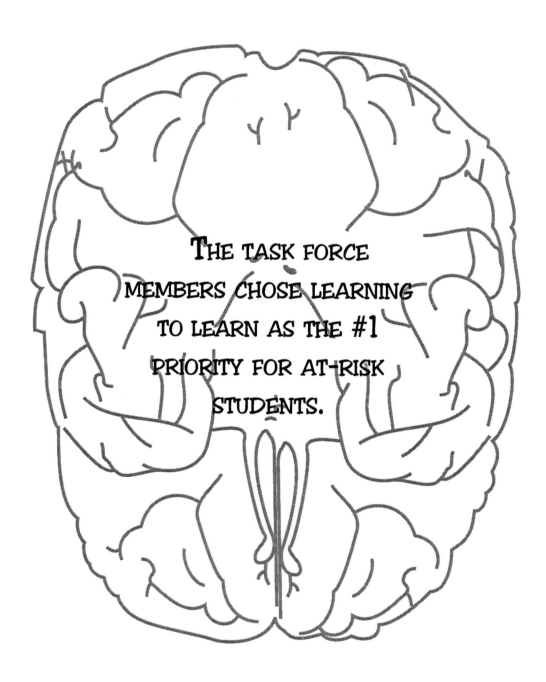

THE TASK FORCE MEMBERS CHOSE LEARNING TO LEARN AS THE #1 PRIORITY FOR AT-RISK STUDENTS.

4) the research and development committee that author Donna co-chaired brought in guest speakers and many articles, books, and films to be read, viewed and discussed for possible inclusion in the final list of recommendations,

5) professional development for guiding learning and thinking provided opportunities for teachers who work with at-risk students, and

6) organizational changes that resulted in a better delivery system for psychological services that focused on prevention, as well as tertiary services, began.

Chapter 8

"True North"
Principles for Teaching
Courageous Learners

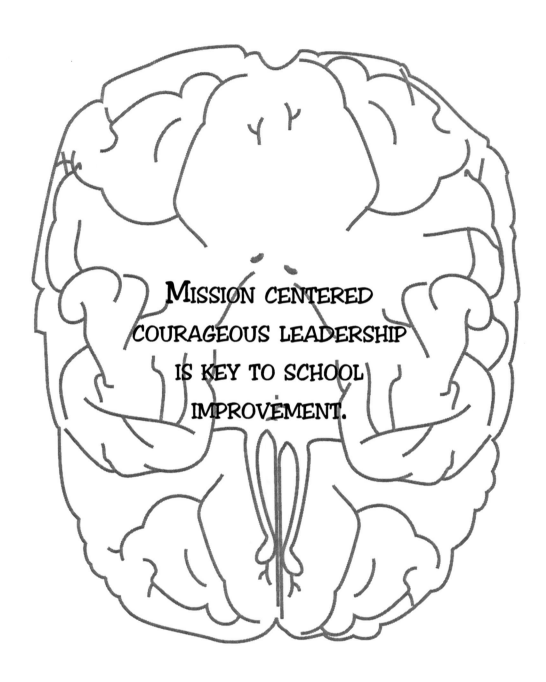

MISSION CENTERED
COURAGEOUS LEADERSHIP
IS KEY TO SCHOOL
IMPROVEMENT.

True North: Mission Centered Leadership

Throughout the thousands of references and hundreds of books that we reviewed putting this work together, one thing became clear. It was as if there was a compass that was always pointing true north towards the true key elements that worked to allow courageous learners to reach their full potential. It is rare in social science for major researchers to agree so strongly about what is likely to work, and what is likely to fail. Fortunately, now with a growing research base, it is a great time to move forward and embrace change on behalf of courageous learners. As mentioned earlier, Deming's work shows us that between 85 and 94 percent of results are produced by the system. Therefore, if we are to keep using the current system of instruction that has failed the majority of courageous learners for the last 50 years, it is unlikely that we will get the results that we want to achieve.

<u>N</u> is for Nurturing a Network of Teacher Leaders

To make a metaphor of a compass pointing True North even more memorable, meaningful, and motivating, we will use a BrainSMART acronym for N.O.R.T.H. The <u>N</u> is for nurturing a network of teacher leaders. It is most encouraging to see the network of teacher leaders who are pioneering the application of what works.

In classrooms across America there are already courageous leaders pioneering the applications of methods of teaching that really work. The greatest danger facing the movement toward allowing our students to become successful is that these highly effective teachers may be driven out of the system. This could happen as they make more standard educators look less than effective. Furthermore, the practice of teaching effectively looks very different from the 1950's classroom when students sat neatly in rows and listened with full attention to a lecture from a teacher before completing quiet, individual, and passive seatwork. As stated earlier there is no research to support long lectures, seatwork, and isolation, followed by occasional pop quizzes as being effective ways for students at-risk to be successful.

The number one job for leaders is to produce change. Author, researcher, and systems expert, Peter Senge (Senge, Cambron-McCabe, Lucas, Smith, Dulton, & Kleiner, 2000), reminds us of some key facts. One, we must stop thinking like mechanics and start acting like gardeners. Two, Senge stated that he had never seen a successful organizational learning program rolled out from the top, not a single one. Usually these programs start with just one team. Senge went on to define leadership as the ability to produce change. We have been inspired as we have worked on this book to meet courageous leaders who demonstrate the ability to produce change by supporting pioneering teacher leaders. These teacher leaders are often educators who are producing

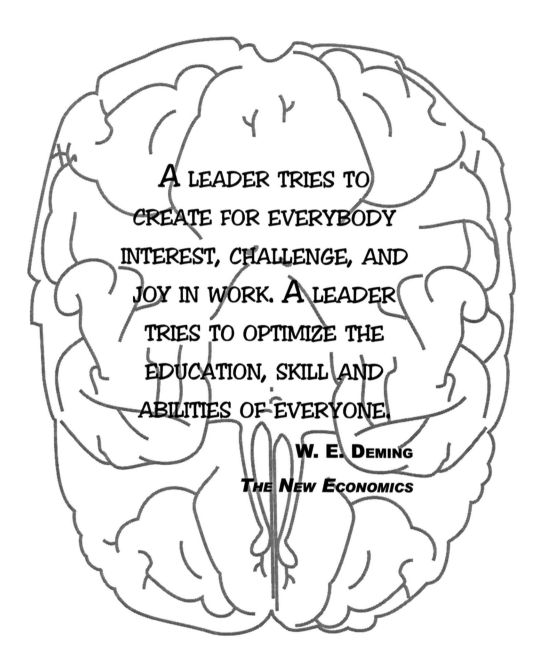

A LEADER TRIES TO
CREATE FOR EVERYBODY
INTEREST, CHALLENGE, AND
JOY IN WORK. A LEADER
TRIES TO OPTIMIZE THE
EDUCATION, SKILL AND
ABILITIES OF EVERYONE.

W. E. DEMING

THE NEW ECONOMICS

results in the classroom by using innovative teaching and research-based techniques.

We would go so far to say that for courageous learners to be successful is primarily dependant on the courage of leaders to facilitate change in teaching practice by nurturing the network of teacher leaders. We have seen this approach work successfully both in the BrainSMART project in Florida and with the Norman Project (Wilson & Church, 1993) in Oklahoma. Leaders must ask themselves, "How well am I supporting the innovative and early adopting teachers within my district?" "If I do not support them how am I expecting positive change to happen?"

O is for Optimism

For us to insure that we lift the learning power of all students, and that we sustain optimism. In other words, it is important that we sustain an optimistic outlook as a result of the specific actions that we are taking. As stated earlier, optimism is a better predictor of success in college than S.A.T. scores. In our workshops when we asked teachers what would happen if all students arrived in their classrooms tomorrow optimistic and with the same level of ability they have, virtually all teachers say there would be a dramatic improvement in learning, student achievement, and test scores.

Here is a question for leaders "How optimistic is my language about courageous learners? What am I actually doing to ensure that teachers raise their expectations of what students at risk can do?" (NOTE: If all I am doing is telling them that all kids can be successful without giving the teachers the tools to do so, I am likely to have a high level of resistance.)

R is for Relationships

If the three laws of real estate are location, location, location, then the three laws of effective teaching are relationship, relationship, and relationship. For courageous learners to have a chance to be successful, it is vital that they have a strong and positive relationship with at least one mature adult. At a time when the average parent spends 7 minutes per week in actual dialogue with their children, it is highly likely that many students arrive in our classrooms without their relationship needs being met. We believe that the ability to relate is not in-born, and that there is a science of relating which is a learnable and teachable set of skills.

Other questions for leaders are, "What am I doing to ensure that every student has a positive and mature adult to relate with? What am I doing right now to make sure all our teachers are equipped with the relating skills they need to assist students in achieving their academic goals?"

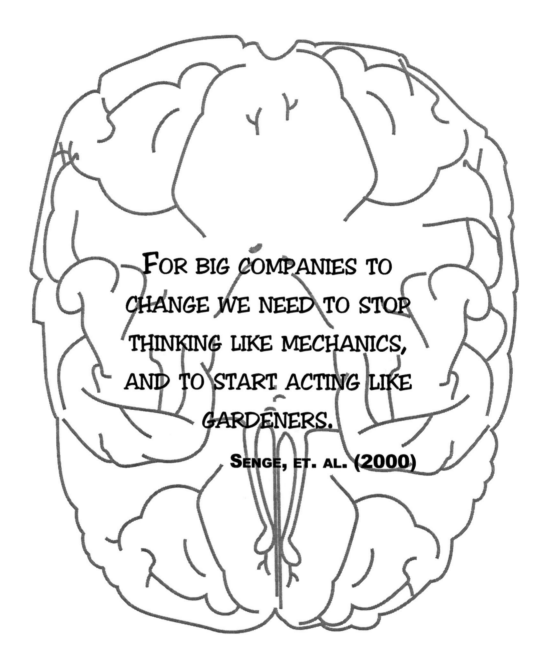

FOR BIG COMPANIES TO
CHANGE WE NEED TO STOP
THINKING LIKE MECHANICS,
AND TO START ACTING LIKE
GARDENERS.

SENGE, ET. AL. (2000)

Researchers conclude that having high expectations is critical for the success of all students. Sadly, much of the feedback that we had from teachers in the field indicates that many teachers do not feel that courageous learners are able to achieve much academic success. This, in our experience, can only be changed by two factors. One, the teachers experience, themselves, through transformational workshops, exactly what effective learning looks, feels, and sounds like. Once they feel empowered as effective learners, they have a much greater belief that their students can also be successful. Two, for teachers to see their own students become more successful as a result of applying their new strategies in the classroom.

T is for Thinking and Learning Tools

Once again, research is consistent in indicating that the thinking and learning tools that students bring to the classroom is the primary determinate of how well they learn and think when they are there. For example, Goodlad's (1984) study of over a thousand classrooms indicated that there was little evidence that students were given the corrective feedback they needed to learn from their mistakes, and often they did not have time to complete tasks. Furthermore, it was often obvious that students did not understand what they were asked to do.

In an international comparison, it is clear in Stigler and Hibert's *The Teaching Gap* (1999), that although American students started similar to those in China or Japan in the first grade, performance began to drop comparatively in second and third grades. We believe a leading cause is not teaching the specific thinking and learning tools that students need to reach a threshold of when they can benefit from classroom activity. If courageous learners do not learn the tools they need, performance will plunge dramatically until eventually at-risk students drop out of school.

The powerful and positive news is that a lot of evidence shows that when we teach the specific thinking and learning tools, virtually all students can be successful in the classroom. The darker news is that the usual solution is often to retain the students in the same grade and repeat the same teaching strategies that failed the first time. When this happens, there is a dramatic increase in the likelihood that the students who have trouble will eventually drop out of school. The research on retention suggests that retention is not an effective remediation process. In addition, the cost of retention is enormous in financial terms, between 5 and 7 thousand dollars per year. Furthermore, in terms of impact on the students, research suggests that only death of a parent or blindness can be more devastating. The equivalent of being retained a grade, in the mind of a student, was more similar to being caught stealing or wetting their pants in the classroom.

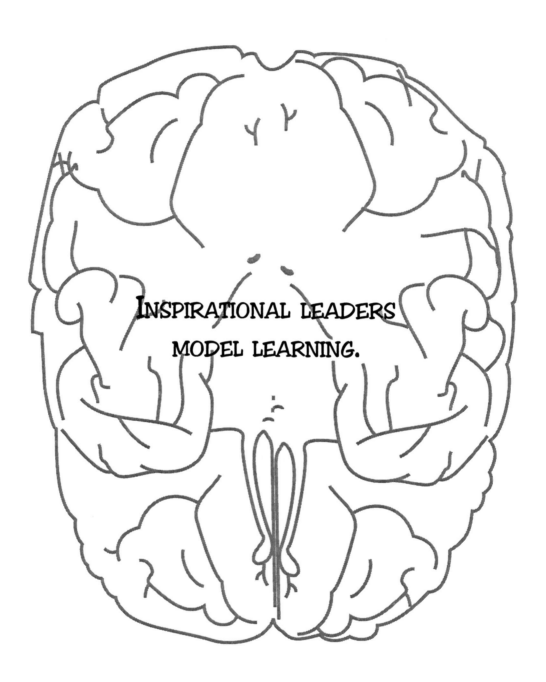

INSPIRATIONAL LEADERS MODEL LEARNING.

Our evidence that teaching specific thinking and learning tools does lead to students success has been a focus of study for cognitive psychologists like Dr. Feuerstein. As earlier mentioned, he and many of his followers have worked with students who have faced horrible life circumstances, however, by learning systematic processes for thinking and learning, students went on to be successful in academics and in life. So, the bottom line is that it can be done. The question is, "Will it be done?".

Questions for leaders are, "How many of my students lack the thinking and learning tools they need to benefit successfully from school? What is my plan to make sure that the students lacking these skills will receive appropriate training to maximizing their probability of success?"

<u>H</u> is for High Expectations

As we mentioned earlier, high expectations of students dramatically increases the probability the students will be successful. What does not work, however, is rhetoric from politicians stating that we demand teachers be held to a higher standard without appropriate systemic support.

RESEARCH BY NASA CONFIRMED THAT CAPTAINS WHO CONSULTED WITH THEIR CREW DURING AN EMERGENCY HAD A HIGHER RATE OF SUCCESS AND SURVIVAL THAT THOSE WHO SIMPLY MADE THEIR OWN DECISIONS.

JAMES O'TOOLE

LEADING CHANGE, 1996

Courageous Leaders: A Call to Action

As we visit classrooms across America, we see teachers being burned out, demoralized, and discouraged by cheap words and insufficient action. The only way that we can truly meet our national goal for all students to achieve academic success is to institute a continuously improving system that ensures every teacher of courageous learners has the tools, training, and time to teach effectively.

Research suggests that today 4 out of 5 teachers do not feel ready to teach effectively in America's classrooms. Furthermore, our belief after seeing the young students who are entering the classrooms, is that the new generation has much higher needs than the previous generation. We also believe that they will respond even more negatively to standard teaching practice than those who came before them. It is important to remember that we are in the midst of a great social experiment which focuses on increasing pressure for performance on standardized tests before we equip teachers and students with the necessary tools and knowledge they need to be successful. Once again, the great news is that we see many excellent examples of quality teaching. When teachers are equipped with highly effective systems of instruction, learning gains follow.

Two questions for leaders are, "What is the prevailing system of instruction for courageous learners in my district? What are some examples of highly effective instruction and what am I doing to nurture the broad application of such practices?"

We are inspired, encouraged, and energized as we see the great work that teachers using highly effective instruction are helping students achieve. The greatest assets that we see are the tremendous courage, commitment, and caring that teachers bring to the classroom every day. We also see the character, hope and trust that courageous learners exhibit just to turn up in classrooms across our land.

Perhaps, most hopefully, we have seen courageous leaders striving for True North in five areas. They are as follows: 1) Nurture the network of teacher leaders so that innovative and instructional techniques are embedded into every day classroom teaching; 2) Leaders speak Optimistically and give students a real reason to believe that they can be successful; 3) Leaders focus on Relationships, relationships, and relationships. They work to make sure the students have mentors. They work with parents, giving support, praise, and strategies to help their children. More importantly, they nurture strong relationships amongst their teachers to help them through the transition from "stand up long lecturing" to "effective teaching;" 4) Leaders focus on making

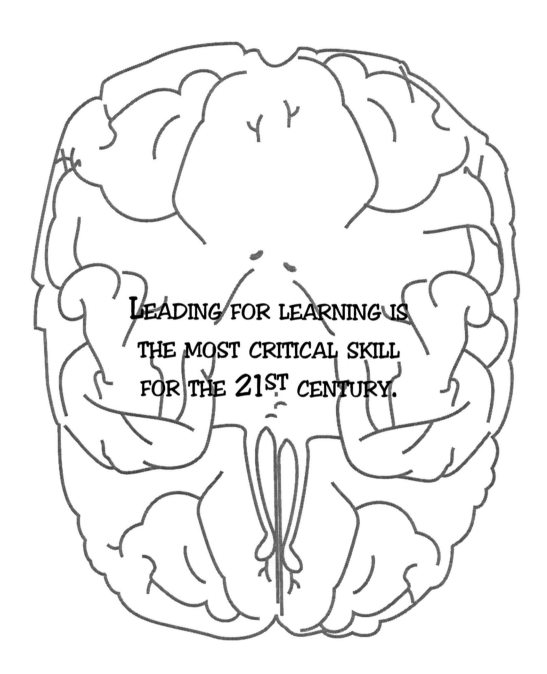

LEADING FOR LEARNING IS
THE MOST CRITICAL SKILL
FOR THE 21ST CENTURY.

sure the students get the <u>T</u>hinking and learning tools they need to be successful. There is large and rapidly growing support from the business community for this, because they desperately need high school graduates who can think, learn, communicate, and work well in teams; and 5) Leaders have <u>H</u>igh expectations based on highly effective teaching. These leaders know that positive expectations flow as a result of effective teachers seeing good results with their students.

The purpose of this book is to honor such courageous leaders, teachers, and the courageous learners who trust us to equip them with the tools that they need to survive and thrive in the 21st Century. We are grateful for the many teachers in classrooms across North America who keep us inspired as we all work toward the mission that *by the year 2020 every child will have the tools to think, learn, communicate, and build healthy, joyful, productive lives.* We hope to be able to support you and the courageous learners in your school district. As you touch the lives of courageous learners, keep your eyes on the prize. You make the difference.

References and Recommended Reading

Courageous Learners: Unleashing the Brain Power of Students from At Risk Situations

Adams, M. (1989). Thinking skills curricula: Their promise and progress. *Educational Psychologist, 24*, 25-27.

Allington, R., & Walmsley, S. (1995). *No quick fix: Rethinking literacy programs in America's elementary schools.* New York: Teachers College Press.

Amen, D. (1998). *Change your brain change your life.* New York: Random House.

American Association of University Women. (1991). *Shortchanging girls, Shortchanging America.* Washington, DC: AAUW.

Anderson, J., Hollinger, D., & Conaty, J. (1993). Reexamining the relationship between school poverty and student achievement. *ERS Spectrum*, 21 -31.

Ayres, A. (1972). *Sensory integration and learning disorders.* Los Angeles: Western Psychological Services.

Beane, J., & Apple, M. (Eds.). (1995). The case for democratic schools. In *Democratic schools.* Alexandria, VA: Association for Supervision and Curriculum Development.

Berg, H., & Conyers, M. (1998). *Speed-reading the easy way.* New York: Barrons.

Blades, J. (2000). *Action based learning: Linking movement to learning.* Paper presented at Eric Jensen's Learning Brain Expo 2000, San Diego, CA.

Bransford, J., Brown, A., & Cocking, R. (Eds.). (1999). *How people learn: Brain, mind, experience, and school.* Washington, DC: National Academy Press.

Buzan, T. (1983). *Use both sides of your brain.* New York: Dutton.

Caine, G., & Caine, R. (1997). *Education on the edge of possibility.* Alexandria: VA: Association for Supervision and Curriculm Development.

Capponi, P. (1997). *Dispatches from the poverty line.* Toronto, Canada: Flenguin Books.

Carnegie Corporation. (Winter 1997). *Not a pretty picture for young children.* In State Education Leader (Vol. 15, 1 pp. 8). Denver, CO: Education Commission of the States.

Carper, J. (2000). *Your miracle brain.* New York: Harper Collins.

Childre, D., Martin, H., & Beech, D. (1999). *The heartmath solution.* New York: Harper Collins.

Comer, J., Haynes, N., Joyner, E., & Ben-Avie, M. (Eds.). (1996). *Rallying the whole village: The Comer process for reforming education.* New York: Teachers College Press.

Conyers, M. (1999). *Mantalk/womenspeak.* Evanston, IL: BrainSMART Publishing.

Conyers, M., & Heverly, L. (1999). *BrainSMART early start.* Orlando, FL: BrainSMART Publishing.

Conyers, M., & Wilson, D. (2000). *BrainSMART strategies for boosting test scores.* Orlando, FL: BrainSMART Publishing.

Cooper, P., & Bilton, K. (Eds.). (1999). ADHD: *Research, practice, and opinion.* London: Whurr Publishers Ltd.

Covey, S. (1989). *The seven habits of highly effective people.* New York: Simon & Schuster.

Crick, F. (1994). *The astonishing hypothesis.* New York: Touchstone Simon & Schuster.

DeBray, R. (1990). Reviewing thought processes in pre-adolescents: towards a dynamic conception of intelligence: *International Journal of Cognitive Education and Mediated Learning, 1,* 211 - 219.

214

Deming, W. (1994). *The new economics for industry, government, and education.* Cambridge, MA: MIT Press.

Dennison, P., & Dennison, G. (1994). *Brain gym* (Rev. Teachers' ed.). Ventura, CA: Edu-Kinesthetics.

Dewey, J. (1938). *Experience and education.* New York: Collier.

Diamond, M. (1988). *Enriching heredity: The impact of the environment on the anatomy of the brain.* New York: Free Press.

Diamond, M., & Hopson, J. (1998) *Magic trees of the mind: How to nurture your child's intelligence, creativity, and healthy emotions from birth through adolescence.* New York: Penguin.

Duncan, G., & Brooks-Gunn, J. (Eds.). (1997). *Consequences of growing up poor.* New York: Russell Sage Foundation.

Duttweiler, P., & Robinson, N. (1999, Fall). *Part of the blueprint for standards-based reform is missing: Where is the foundation?* (Special Report, #2). Clemson, SC: Clemson University National Dropout Prevention Center.

Eisner, E. (1994). *Cognition and curriculum reconsidered.* New York: Teachers College Press.

Elias, M. (November 30, 1999). Depressing trend: Eroding support for kids. *U.S.A. Today.*

Emerson, L. (1986). Feuerstein's cognitive education theory and American Indian education. Paper presented at the Mediated Learning Experience International Workshop, Jerusalem, Israel.

Fern, V., Anstrom, K., & Silcox, B. (1993). Active learning and the limited English proficient student. *Directions in language and education: National clearinghouse for bilingual education* [On-line]. *1.* Available: http://www.ncbe.gwu.edu/ncbepubs/directions/dirl2.html.

Feuerstein, R., Klien, P., & Tannenbaum, A. (1991). *Mediated learning experience (MLE) theoretical, psychosocial, and learning implications.* London: Freund Publishing House, Ltd.

Feuerstein, R. (1980). *Instrumental enrichment.* Baltimore, MD: University Park Press.

Feuerstein, R., Klien, P., & Tannenbaum, A. (1991). *Mediated learning esperience (MLE) theoretical, psychosocial, and learning implications.* London: Freund.

Feuerstein, R., Rand, Y., & Hoffman, M. (1979). *The dynamic assessment of retarded performers: the learning potential assessment device, theory instruments and techniques.* Baltimore MD: University Park Press.

Fogarty, R. (1997). *Problem-based learning and other curriculum models for the multiple intelligences classroom.* Arlington Heights, IL: SkyLight.

Frankl, V. (1984). *Man's search for meaning.* (3rd ed.). New York: Simon & Schuster.

Friend, M., & Bursuck, W. (1996). *Including students with special needs: A practical guide for classroom teachers.* Needham Heights, MA: Allyn Bacon.

Fuller, R. (1977). *In search of the I.Q. correlation: A scientific whodunit.* Stony Brook, NY: BALL-STICK-BIRD Publications.

Gardner, H. (1983). *Frames of mind: the theory of multiple intelligences.* New York: Bantam Books.

Glig, J. (1990). The use of mediated learning to enhance the educational effectiveness of school programs for high-risk youth. *International Journal of Cognitive Education and Mediated Learning, 1,* 63-71.

Goodlad, J. (1984). *A place called school.* New York: McGraw-Hill.

Golman, D. (1995). *Emotional intelligence.* New York: Bantam Books.

Greenberg, B. (1999). *Stress management: How to improve performance, motivation, and behavior.* Paper presented at the conference of the Public Information Resources, Inc., Boston, MA.

Grinder, M. (1991). *Righting the educational conveyor belt.* Portland, OR: Metamorphous Press.

Grossman, H., & Grossman, S. (1994). *Gender issues in education.* Boston: Allyn-Bacon.

Guskey, T. (1994). Teacher efficacy : A study of construct dimensions. *American Educational Research Journal, 31,* 627-641.

Haberman, M. (1995). *Star teachers of children in poverty.* Madison, WI: Phi Delta Kappa.

Hannaford, C. (1995). *Smart moves.* Arlington, VA: Great Ocean.

Hannaford, C. (1997): *The dominance factor.* Arlington, VA: Great Ocean.

Hart, L. (1983). *Human brain and human learning.* New York: Longman.

Healy, J. (1990). *Endangered minds: Why our children don't think and what we can do about it.* New York: Simon and Schuster.

Hilliard, A. (1987). The learning potential assessment device and instrumental enrichment as a paradigm shift. *The Negro Educational Review, 38,* 200 - 208.

Irlen, H. (1991*). Reading by the colors: Overcoming dyslexia and other reading disabilities through the Irlen method.* Garden City Park, New York: Avery.

Jensen, E. (2000). *Different brains, different learners.* San Diego, CA: The Brain Store.

Jung, C. (1971). In W. McGuire, H. Read, M. Fordham, & G. Adler (Eds.). and R.F.C. Hull (Trans.), *Collected works: Psychological types.* Number XX Bollingen Series. Princeton, NJ: Princeton University Press.

Kaplen, L., & Edelfelt, R. (Eds.). (1996). *Teachers for the new millennium: Aligning teacher development, national goals, and high standards for all students.* Thousand Oaks, CA: Corwin Press.

Koch, R. (1998). *The 80/20 principle: The secret of achieving more with less.* New York: Doubleday.

Kohn, A. (1999). *The schools our children deserve: Moving beyond traditional classrooms and "tougher standards."* New York: Houghton-Mifflin.

Kotulak, R. (1996). *Inside the brain: Revolutionary discoveries of how the mind works.* Kansas City, MO: Universal Press Syndicate.

Kozol, J. (1991). *Savage inequalities.* New York: Harper Perennial.

Kozol, J. (1995). *Amazing Grace.* New York: Crown.

Kozulin, A., & Rand, Y. (Eds.). (2000). *Experience of mediated learning: An impact of Feuerstein's theory in education and psychology.* New York: Pergamon.

Kronenberg, B. (1990). Feuerstein's structural cognitive modifiability (SCM) and psychotherapy at a school for physically disabled pupils. *International Journal of Cognitive Education and Mediated Learning, 1,* 171-177.

Kubler-Ross, E. (1969). *On death and dying.* New York: Macmillan.

LeDoux, J. (1996). *The emotional brain: The mysterious underpinnings of emotional life.* New York: Simon & Schuster.

Lewis, A. (1996). Breaking the cycle of poverty. *Phi Delta Kappan.* 78.

Longo, P. (1999). *Distributed knowledge in the brain: Using visual thinking to improve student learning.* Paper presented at the conference of the Public Information Resources, Inc., Boston, MA.

Martin, D. (1997, March). *Mediated learning experience and deaf learners.* Paper presented at the 3rd International Conference on Teaching for Intelligence, Vancouver, British Columbia.

Meier, D. (2000). *The accelerated learning handbook: a creative guide to designing and delivering faster, more effective training programs.* New York: McGraw-Hill.

Merzenich, M., et al. (1993). Neural mechanisms underlying temporal integration, segmentation, and input sequence representation: Some implications for the origin of learning disabilities. *Annals of the New York Academy of Sciences, 682,* 1-22.

Miller, G. (1956). The magical number seven, plus or minus two: Some limits on our capacity for processing information. *The Psychological Review, 63,* 81-97.

National Education Commission on Time and Learning. (1994). *Prisoners of time report.* Washington, D.C.

Norwood, R. (1985). *Women who love too much.* Los Angeles: Tarcher.

Olenchak, F. (1995). Effects of enrichment on gifted/learning disabled students. *Journal of Education of the Gifted, 18,* 385-399.

Ornstein, R., & Thompson, R. (1984). *The amazing brain.* Boston: Houghton Mifflin.

O'Toole, J. (1996). *Leading change: The argument for values-based leadership.* New York: Jossey-Bass.

Perkins, D. (1992). *Smart schools: Better thinking and learning for every child. New* York: Free Press.

Perkins, D. (1995). *Outsmarting IQ: The emerging science of learnable intelligence.* New York: Free Press.

Pert, C. (1999). *Molecules of emotion.* (2nd ed.). New York: Touchstone.

Peskin, B., & Conyers, M. (2000). *Peak performance and radiant health: Moving beyond the zone.* Houston, TX: Noble.

Presseisen, B. (1986). *Critical thinking and thinking skills: State of the art definitions and practice in public schools.* Philadelphia: Research for Better Schools.

Presseisen, B. (1988). *At risk students and thinking perspectives from research.* Washington, DC: National Education Association.

Ratey, J. (1999). *The care and feeding of the brain.* Paper presented at the conference of the Public Information Resources, Inc., Boston, MA.

Resnick, L., & Klopfer, L. (1989). *Toward the thinking curriculum: Current cognitive research* (1989 Yearbook.). Alexandria, VA: Association for Supervision and Curriculum Development.

Reynolds, D., & Teddlie, C. (2000). An introduction to school effectiveness research. In Teddlie, C. & Reynolds, D (Eds.), *The international handbook of school effectiveness research.* (pp. 3-25). London: Falmer Press.

Roizen, M. (1999). *Real age: Are you as young as you can be?* New York: Harper-Collins.

Samuelson, R. (1997). The culture of poverty. *Newsweek. Vol. 129,*

Sapolsky, R. (1998). *Why zebras don't get ulcers.* New York: Freeman.

Satir, V. (1978). *Your many faces.* Millbrae, CA: Celestial Arts.

Satir, V. (1988). *The new peoplemaking.* Mountain View, CA: Science & Behavior Books.

Secretary's Commission on Achieving Necessary Skills (SCANS). (1991). *What work requires of schools: A SCANS report for America 2000.* Washington, DC: U.S. Department of Labor.

Seligman, M. (1995). *The optimistic child.* New York: Harper-Collins.

Senge, P., Cambron-McCabe, N., Lucas, T., Smith, B., Dutton, J., & Kleiner, A. (1999). *The dance of change: The challenges to sustaining momentum in learning organizations.* New York: Doubleday.

Senge, P., Cambron-McCabe, N., Lucas, T., Smith, B., Dutton, J., & Kleiner, A. (2000). *Schools that learn: A fifth discipline fieldbook for educators, parents, and everyone who cares about education.* New York: Doubleday.

Sharron, H. (1987). *Changing children's minds: Feuerstein's revolution in the teaching of intelligence.* London: Souvenir Press.

Siegel, D. (1999). *The developing mind: Toward a neurobiology of interpersonal experience.* New York: Guilford.

Somer, E. (1995). *Food and mood: How the nutrients in food improve memory, energy levels, sleep patterns, weight management, and attitude.* New York: Holt.

Soska, M. (1994). Educational technology enhances LEP classroom. *Forum* [On-line serial], 17 (5). Available: http: //www.ncbe.gwu.edu/ncbe/forum/forum175.html.

Sousa, D. (1995). *How the brain learns.* Reston, VA: National Association Secondary School Principals.

Springer, S., & Deutsch, G. (1998). *Left brain right brain.* New York: Freeman.

Stainback, S., & Stainback, W. (1992). *Teaching in inclusive classroom communities: Curriculum design, adaptation, and delivery.* Baltimore: Brookes.

Sternberg, R. (1997). *Successful intelligence.* New York: Simon & Schuster.

Stevenson, H., & Stigler, J. (1992). *The learning gap: Why our schools are failing and what we can learn from Japanese and Chinese education.* New York: Simon-Schuster.

Stigler, J., & Hiebert, J. (1999). *The teaching gap: Best ideas from the world's teachers for improving education in the classroom.* New York: Free Press.

Sylwester, R. (1995). *A celebration of neurons: An educator's guide to the brain.* Alexandria, VA: Association of Supervision and Curriculum Development.

Sylwester, R. (2000). *A biological brain in a cultural classroom: Applying biological research to classroom management.* Thousand Oaks, CA: Corwin Press.

Tallal, P. (1994). In the perception of speech, time is of the essence. In G.Buzsaki, et al. (Eds.), *Temporal codings in the brain* (pp. 291-299). Berlin: Springer-Verlag.

Vygotsky, L. (1978). *Mind in society.* Cambridge, MA: Harvard University Press.

Walberg, H. (1988). Productive educational practices for at-risk youth. In Council of Chief State School Officers (Eds.). *School success for students at-risk* (pp. 175-194). Chicago: Harcourt-Brace-Jovanovich.

Wang, M., Haertel, G., & Walberg, H. (1993). Toward a knowledge base for school learning. *Review of Educational Research, 63,* 249-294.

Washington, V., & Andrews, J. (Eds.). (1998). The knowledge base: Diversity, change, and opportunity. In *Children of 2010.* Washington, DC: National Association for the Education of Young Children.

Wegscheider, S. (1981). *Another chance: Hope and health for alcoholic families.* Palo Alto, CA: Science & Behavior Books.

Weinstein, E., & Rosen, E. (1999). *Teaching children about health: A multidisciplinary approach.* Englewood, CA: Morton.

Wheatley, M. (1992). *Leadership and the new science.* San Francisco: Berrett-Koehler.

Wigle, S., & Wilcox, D. (1996). "Inclusion: Criteria for the preparation of education personnel. *Remedial and Special Education, 17,* 323-328.

Wilson, D., & Church, S. (1993). Norman public schools' three year study of at-risk students. Published in *Teaching Thinking and Problem Solving, , .* Philadelphia: Research in Better Schools Publication.

Wilson, D. (1996). The school psychologist as co-teacher: An example using COGNET Program as a means of teaching thinking skills". *Journal of Cognitive Education, Vol. 5,* 171 -183.

Wilson, D., & Conyers, M. (in press, a). *BrainSMART in the house: Learning for school, learning for life.* Orlando, FL: BrainSMART Publishing.

Winson, D., & Conyers, M. (in press, b). *BrainSMART thinking for results!* Orlando, FL: BrainSMART Publishing.

Wolfe, P. (1994). *A staff developer's guide to the brain.* (Cassette recordings). Front Royal, VA: National Cassette Services.

Wolffe, R., & Robinson, H. (2000). *Connect Learning Through Movement.* Paper presented at Eric Jensen's Learning Brain Expo 2000, San Diego, CA.

Wurtman, J. (1986). *Managing your mind and mood through food.* New York: Harper-Row.

Zavacky, F. *Connecting the curriculum through movement.* Paper presented at Eric Jenson's Learning Brain Expo 2000, San Diego, CA.